TOOTH & CLAW

TOOTH &CLAW
THE DINOSAUR WARS

Deborah Noyes

Viking

VIKING

An imprint of Penguin Random House LLC

375 Hudson Street

New York, New York 10014

First published in the United States of America by Viking,
an imprint of Penguin Random House LLC, 2019

LIBRARY OF CONGRESS CATALOGING-IN-PUBLICATION DATA IS AVAILABLE

ISBN: 9780425289846

Manufactured in China   Set in ITC Veljovic Std   Book design by Kate Renner

10 9 8 7 6 5 4 3 2 1

For Clyde—

once a proud (and certified) member of the Dinosaur Society

CONTENTS

The Terrible Lizard of New Jersey

Today we take it for granted that massive creatures once roamed the earth, swam the oceans, and wheeled in the skies.

Biologically, they were both like and unlike some of the millions of species alive today.

With images of prehistoric life all around us, it's easy to see these extinct giants—and their lost worlds—in our mind's eye. Today dinosaurs sing toddlers to sleep at nap time. They lock horns in video games. They decorate everything from lunch boxes to company logos. What's harder to imagine is a time *before* all that, a time when no one knew that dinosaurs had ever existed, much less what one might *look* like.

Remains unearthed in England in the nineteenth century began to offer scientists tantalizing clues that massive reptilian creatures had once prowled the planet. But in the scientific community, too, the word "dinosaur"—from the ancient Greek for "terrible" and "lizard"—was still new. It had only begun rattling around Europe in 1842, when British anatomist Richard Owen coined the term after comparing a range of fossils.

Under Owen's guidance, a group of life-size reconstructions had been designed and sculpted for the grounds of the restored Crystal Palace at Sydenham, England, unveiled in 1854.

But the exotic giants in that attraction, which drew more than forty thousand people on opening day, owed more to the vision of British natural

The first mounted dinosaur, Hadrosaurus foulkii, *with artist-sculptor*
Benjamin Waterhouse Hawkins, 1868.

history artist Benjamin Waterhouse Hawkins, under Owen's somewhat out-dated direction, than to paleontology.

If Hawkins's models stretched the truth—only suggesting the Iguanodons and Megalosaurs they portrayed—it was because the anatomist and the artist had so little to work from. In the early 1850s, dinosaur finds were still scarce. Nothing approaching a complete skeleton had been dug up yet. Most fossil collections were dusty boxes of loose teeth and bones, of interest only to specialists.

While scientists were logging new finds, learning to fit together the remains of extinct animals, and musing over the larger puzzle, Philadelphia's Academy of Natural Sciences—which at the time had the most complete dinosaur specimen known to science—did something that would thrust the growing science of paleontology into the spotlight.

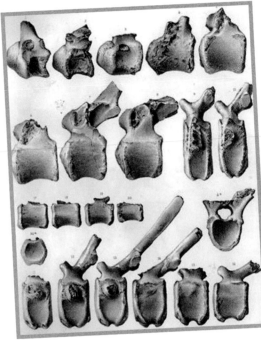

Plate from Joseph Leidy's description of Hadrosaurus, *1865.*

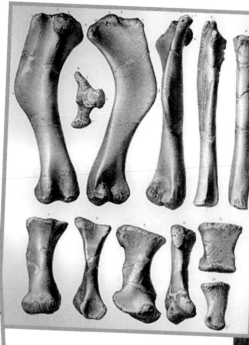

TEN YEARS AND A CIVIL WAR HAD PASSED SINCE THE ORGANIZATION'S FOSSILS of *Hadrosaurus foulkii* were hauled out of the mud in southern New Jersey, but if bones could speak—and they do, with help—they would tell a story millions of years old. So Philadelphia's academy hired Benjamin Waterhouse Hawkins to fashion the world's first fully articulated dinosaur skeleton.

Hawkins began work on the landmark exhibit in September 1868.

Guided by Dr. Joseph Leidy, who had first described and introduced *Hadrosaurus foulkii* into the scientific record a decade before—and Leidy's young protégé, Edward Drinker Cope—the artist worked at a feverish pace to suspend plaster casts of old bones from a metal armature.

Hadrosaurus was a fair portion of a thirty-foot herbivore, but there were still bones missing. Hawkins shaped plaster reconstructions for these; and since no skull had been found at the New Jersey dig site, the artist invented one, basing it on the head of an iguana.

When the academy in Philadelphia unveiled Hawkins's masterpiece two short months later, it would set the standard for museum displays around the

NAMING THE BEAST

Though *Hadrosaurus* was the first close-to-complete dinosaur skeleton found and the first mounted, the first fossil had been recorded way back in 1676 by Robert Plot, an English museum curator. Though he believed the thighbone he drew was a human giant's, it probably belonged to a megalosaur.

In 1824, *Megalosaurus bucklandii* was described and named after William Buckland (1784-1856), a British fossil hunter and clergyman. (Though fossil hunters Gideon and Mary Ann Mantell found the *Iguanodon* first, the specimen was described later.) Other finds in 1822 and 1833 kept interest in fossils brewing, but it wasn't until British anatomist Richard Owen (1804-92) sat down to study and compare the available bones that science created a class distinct from living reptiles.

In 1842 Owen published his study, naming the extinct creatures "Dinosauria" ("terrible lizard" or "fearfully great reptile").

globe. Before this 1868 event, very few could have imagined the beast upright in skeletal form in the gallery, much less ponder its sizable remains. Proof of prehistoric life on a grand scale, the twenty-six-foot-long skeleton suggested a globe once teeming with mysterious monsters.

For the sedate academy, the fanfare that followed was a mixed blessing. In an average year, the institution accommodated thirty thousand visitors. The year after *Hadrosaurus* opened, it squeezed in sixty-six thousand; the following year a hundred thousand.

Dr. Leidy's plan to expand "the minds of the masses" and "advance science" by exposing more people to natural history hadn't exactly backfired, but the building simply couldn't contain the press of crowds from around the world.

Eager, noisy, and jostling, they kicked up dust, endangered rare fossil collections, and—complained the academy secretary in a year-end report— caused "many accidents" and "considerable destruction of property." The damage included broken glass, ruined woodwork, and that infernal dust, which settled over horizontal display cases and blocked the view.

The academy began charging admission to discourage all but serious visitors, but with so many clamoring for a look at the world's first mounted dinosaur, the beleaguered institution had to rally funds for a new home—twice as big—for its terribly popular terrible lizard.

HADROSAURUS INTRODUCED A HUNGRY PUBLIC TO THE DINOSAURS OF NORTH America but only hinted at the bounty to come.

Dino mania was officially on, and few would play a bigger role in the race to discover monster-sized species than Dr. Leidy's brilliant and temperamental young employee, Edward Drinker Cope. A rising star in the young field of paleontology, the twenty-nine-year-old "bone hound" would soon make an embarrassing mistake and a powerful enemy.

But he would also make history.

Kind regards of E. D. Cope
5 – 1876

The Prodigy

"I am not constructed for getting along comfortably with the general run of people."

—E. D. COPE, IN A LETTER TO HIS FATHER

When Edward was a little boy, his father, Alfred, taught him a rhyme:

Pigs have bristles,
Cows have hair,
Birds have feathers,
Snakes are bare.

A devout Quaker, the elder Cope had strong ideas about how his son should be raised and educated. But from a tender age, the unusually spirited (Alfred might argue willful) Edward had his own ideas. Prone to "incessant activity" of mind and body, the boy "reached in every direction for

Edward Drinker Cope, 1870.

knowledge." His memory was almost photographic, and he expressed his thoughts in a "bright and merry way." Even as a child, he wouldn't be contained or corralled.

Though he lost his mother at just three years old, Edward's new stepmother took to him and his sisters warmly. He enjoyed a large extended family and, as the son of a wealthy Quaker, the social and educational support of Philadelphia's Society of Friends. For Edward, knowledge was everywhere, and ever within reach. Philadelphia at the time was America's second-largest city and a cultural and scientific center rivaled only by Boston.

Artist Charles Willson Peale. Tickets to his Philadelphia museum bore the slogan "The Birds & Beasts will teach thee," words young Cope took to heart.

Edward was only six when he began recording his observations of nature in journals, letters, and drawings. "I saw Mammoth," he reported in a note to his grandmother, after a visit to the Peale Museum, "and Hydrarchus." Did she know what that was? "It is a great skeleton of a serpent. It was so long that it had to be put in three rooms. There was a stuffed crocodile, and an alligator, and the crocodile looked the ugliest and fiercest," he added, with the joyful curiosity and earnest passion for the natural world that endeared him to people all his life.

Another time, Edward wrote and illustrated a little hand-sewn journal of a birthday voyage by boat to Boston with Alfred. "We saw some Bonetas swimming along-side the vessel," he reported. "They're long slim fish and twist about like eels. We saw a Man-of-war, which looked like a large jelly-fish only he was dead. The night before we saw a great many lights in the water which were made by Jellyfish and here is a picture of it."

In 1849, Edward began attending a Philadelphia Quaker day school and became a regular at the Academy of Natural Sciences. He described the museum treasures he saw there—"several small skulls of birds of different sizes and forms"—as he might do years later, as an adult curator. He loved drafting maps and geographical studies.

By the time Alfred sent him to a Quaker boarding school in Westtown, Pennsylvania, in 1853, Edward was advanced—

sides. One came close along side of the ves-sel The captain ran and got a harpoon to catch one, but it was too late They had all swam away.

FIGURE 2.

A page from the notebook of Edward Cope, age 7, on a birthday voyage to Boston with his father.

and cocky—enough to feel let down by his teachers. In one letter home, he gloated over the scientific name of a species of turtle that "Master Davis" had failed to identify.

At Westtown, Edward favored languages, especially Greek, as well as mathematics and chemistry, but he liked sledding, ice-skating, and "corner ball" more. He was an erratic student, and Alfred urged him to do better. Edward had his reasons, excuses, and explanations, and while he was at Westtown, real tension mounted between father and son.

At the center of this clash of wills were Alfred's plans for his son. A godly man and a gentleman farmer, Alfred hoped to shepherd his boy into a comparable future, modeled on that of the third president of the United States.

Like Thomas Jefferson, like Alfred himself, Edward could expect a life of relative leisure, a modest and noble one devoted to the care and cultivation of the good earth.

After Edward turned thirteen, Alfred loaned his son out to friends and associates each summer, fellow Pennsylvania landowners who would continue to teach the young man the ins and outs of his family business. Alfred hoped to tame his privileged and high-strung boy and impress on him the value of hard work, but Edward had a restless temper.

"Work, work, work," he complained at fifteen, "every day after day, I have no fancy for it."

Edward saw farming as a waste of time. He wanted to be a biologist. He may have resented them, but his farm summers nourished his intense love of nature. He found time to roam the woods and streams of Chester County, observing forest birds, swamp flowers, and field snakes and turning over mossy stones in search of salamanders. He bristled at farm labor, but his hands and mind were far from lazy.

In a letter written in his teens, he praised a cousin who shared his "admiration of nature and detail," an appreciation "heightened, not chilled, by the necessary 'investigation.'" People liked a nice view, he complained, but couldn't care less about the wondrous processes behind the scenes. They were afraid to get dirty, and they winced at frogs. He even hinted that it might be best to keep his enthusiasm for a particular salamander species hush-hush to avoid ridicule.

When he wasn't out exploring, he pursued his natural gift for languages, even coaxing Alfred to hire him a tutor, but native brilliance didn't make him a good student. When bored, as he often was, Edward was prone to mischief. His letters home from boarding school are full of tangled lines of defense against his father's disapproval.

At the end of 1855, a low conduct mark at Westtown infuriated Alfred. "A public disgrace what can he mean?" the fifteen-year-old complained in a letter to one of his two sisters. "I'm sure I've done nothing to merit it *this* session at any rate. . . . I don't think I've been guilty of any more than one—if that—act of willful disorder."

He scoffed at his father's judgment of him as a "wicked boy," arguing that "laughing a little too loud and a great many little things can go together, and make a bad conduct number" and also, somewhat desperately, "I am sure there has been no ill will or feeling between any teacher and myself."

Whatever the outcome of the skirmish, Edward's formal education ended abruptly at age sixteen. Instead, he stepped up his self-education, nourishing a few years of formal schooling with direct study of nature and tireless inquiry. By his late teens, prowling field, stream, and forest—and the halls of the academy museum—had made him an expert on lizards and snakes.

In 1860, at age twenty, the son known for "great independence in character and action" took a deep breath and asked his father to let him attend Joseph Leidy's anatomy classes at the University of Pennsylvania. "The whole ground is gone over in winter," he argued—Alfred still clung to the idea that Edward would be a farmer—and "knowledge of human and comparative anatomy would be of immense service," he added slyly, to a farmer "desiring a knowledge of the proper manner of treating stock."

Alfred gave in, no doubt exasperated. Their struggle caused both men anguish over the years. Edward was a devoted son and, as long as his father lived, respected him as an intellectual confidant; but however much he loved nature and country life, he couldn't see himself bound to the land.

"I have been hoe-harrowing corn," Edward complained once—trying to reason with the patriarch on practical terms—"and the thought occurred to me several times as I walked slowly back and forward across the field—how much more money could a man make by applying himself to some other business."

While the farmer "pokes backward and forward across his field, earning nothing beyond the cutting of a few weeds," he ventured, the scientist might discover countless new species or otherwise prove himself productive in the field of his choice.

For Alfred, it was a losing battle.

Over time and without meaning to—as the little rhyme about pigs and snakes reveals—Alfred had taught Edward to look and listen. He'd taught him to sort and classify. He'd taught him to think like a scientist.

In the end, Alfred Cope had given his fiery son the tools he needed to thwart his father's will.

Joseph Leidy lecturing on anatomy, 1887.

DREAMING OF STRANGE FORMS

Dr. Joseph Leidy was a professor of anatomy at the University of Pennsylvania medical school when he hired Edward Drinker Cope to help him catalog the academy's collections.

A Philadelphian from birth, Leidy was educated as a doctor but was too shy and modest to succeed in practice. According to one biographer, the anatomist-in-training was "so revolted by his first human dissection that he fled and did not return [to class] for six weeks. It took a year for him to overcome his 'melancholy,'" though Leidy would

EDWARD'S OBSESSIVE KNOWLEDGE AND PASSION FOR SCIENCE DIDN'T VEX OR ESCAPE the observant Dr. Leidy. His anatomy teacher urged him to join the Academy of Natural Sciences. While Dr. Leidy documented dinosaur anatomy, young Cope recataloged the museum's collection of reptile and amphibian skeletons.

By 1861, at age twenty-one, Edward had finished work on the collection and presented his first paper on salamanders at an academy meeting. He was elected a full member of the academy and the following year clocked seven more scientific papers.

He was well on his way to prominence, but there was one small problem: his personality.

Cope could easily lapse into biting sarcasm. He was a brooder, a mental scrapper with little patience for erroneous thinking, and could turn intense in even cheerful disputes. There was something warlike in his nature, Leidy observed, and some found him brash, unsettling, or just exasperating (though he made academy meetings lively).

While Cope's boss and mentor was a mild conservative, a master of precise detail who never hurried and rarely speculated, Cope was daring, abrupt,

eventually teach anatomy himself. Live patients proved just as trying: when he caught sight of his first coming up the walk to his home office, Leidy bolted the door and retreated to a back room. Zoology and comparative anatomy were a happy compromise. "You can have no idea how much my mind has become inflamed on this subject," Leidy told a colleague in 1851. "Night after night I dream of strange forms: Eocene crania with recent eyes in them."

This intense engagement with fossil life surely influenced his eager young assistant: Cope would one day be praised for his imaginative views of prehistory.

Leidy named the first US dinosaur from teeth recovered in an 1856 expedition to Montana. His book *The Extinct Mammalian Fauna of Dakota and Nebraska* and his 1858 description of *Hadrosaurus foulkii* would establish him as the country's first professional paleontologist and the go-to expert on North American fossils.

and combative. Despite Cope's limited formal education, Leidy readily acknowledged the younger man's brilliance and trusted Cope implicitly with the care of the academy's precious collections. However, he freely admitted, "he does things in an unnecessarily offensive manner."

Cope's swagger on the job or out in the smoky, hushed dens of gentlemen's scientific clubs rubbed his peers the wrong way. Once, after a fistfight with a friend in the elegant marble lobby of the American Philosophical Society—a lofty institution founded by Benjamin Franklin and others back in 1743—another friend noted his black eye and asked what happened. Cope's retort, along the lines of "you should see the other guy," was no exaggeration.

Abrasive or not, Cope also had the power to charm or outright enchant. He could be a jolly companion, and his charisma got him out of scrapes and attracted loyal followers, as did his magnetic vision of the natural world. He looked deeply and profoundly into the ancient past, so much so that friends and followers were sometimes taken aback by his hypnotic musings.

Still determined to tame his son's ambitions and bind him to the land, Alfred bought Edward a farm called McShag's Pinnacle in rural Chester County, Pennsylvania.

In 1861, Edward wasted no time renting out house and land and fleeing to Washington, DC, to continue his research at the Smithsonian museum. "I have very interesting times talking to the various learned persons who haunt this place," he told one of his sisters. "I can learn something every second."

Life at the Smithsonian was stimulating in more ways than one. The mood was mischievous in those days, with young scientists boarding on the premises and participating in a fair deal of drinking and carousing (as well as raucous footraces through the institution's Great Hall). The merriment extended outdoors to a bustling gaslit town on the brink of war, and the capital's active social life swept Cope into an unsuitable love affair. Little is known about this romance—he purposely destroyed any paper trail—but it took its toll.

Within months of his arrival, Confederate forces opened fire on Fort

Smithsonian Institution, Washington, DC, circa 1864.

Sumter and the Civil War began. News from the front was bleak. A Quaker with supposedly pacifist principles, Cope thought about serving as a field hospital orderly, but Leidy—who began his career as a doctor but had no stomach for the gory truths of medicine—talked him out of it. Alfred was an abolitionist, and Edward weighed the possibility also of teaching emancipated slaves in the South. But as the war wore on, he kept commuting between Philadelphia and Washington, retreating to bones and specimens. He worked and studied hard over the next few years, pursuing whatever natural history topics—living and fossil—fired his mind, and as a result, his education was haphazard or old-fashioned, less specialized than that of many of his contemporaries.

To shield his son from the draft (and perhaps to wrench him from his bad romance with a belle outside accepted social circles), Alfred agreed to fund an excursion to Europe.

Heartsick, with his "sensibilities scorched into a crust," Edward found himself crossing the Atlantic with letters of introduction to some of Europe's great scientists. He would "crowd out painful thoughts" by touring museums and private collections in England, Belgium, Germany, Italy, France, and Switzerland.

"If I know myself I need every possible aid to distract myself from myself," he wrote from London in 1864, revealing fears for his health and well-being. If he didn't stay busy, his story wouldn't end well: "I do not much doubt, in insanity."

Along the tour, when despair took hold, Cope destroyed notes, sketches, and letters, but a record remains of his meeting, in Germany, with another ambitious young paleontologist.

Othniel Charles Marsh was studying at the University of Berlin that year. The two were wildly different, but their professional friendship flourished on strange soil—two young Americans abroad, inspired by Europe's scientific riches. They were probably each aware, too, of the advantages and opportunities waiting back home as the US Civil War wound down and the country spread rapidly west.

Marsh may not have commented on it at the time, but he definitely took note of the emotional and mental states of his new colleague and friend. Years later, when things had soured between them, he would tell the press, "Professor Cope called upon me [in Berlin] and with great frankness confided to me some of the many troubles that even then beset him. My sympathy was aroused, and although I had some doubts of his sanity, I gave him good advice and was willing to be his friend."

Professional friendship seemed a given—in this context of youthful discovery, at a time when very few others were pursuing the same path—but given how quickly the blade of rivalry later came between them, they must have scrutinized each other plenty in Berlin. Paleontology was a bold new science, and the pressure on each man to make a name for himself quickly, and before the other guy, would have been intense.

Marsh had already earned two university degrees by this time but had published only two scientific papers. Cope, with no degrees, had churned out thirty-seven scientific papers in five years. Was Marsh intimidated by this self-taught prodigy from an old Philadelphia family? Or did the practical scholar see Cope as flighty, an amateur? Did Cope look down on the rough-edged Marsh (despite a famously wealthy uncle, Marsh had a stark childhood and lacked social charms) or envy the older man's stability and connections?

The friends went their separate ways but began bouncing manuscripts, fossils, and letters with "kind regards" back and forth.

Home in Philadelphia, Cope took up a post teaching zoology at Haverford College. He soon countered his disastrous DC romance with a stable, approved marriage to a distant cousin who had been raised and educated in the Quaker tradition. Annie Pim was "an amiable woman, not over sensitive, with considerable energy." Perhaps key, with recent history in mind: she was "inclined to be serious," not to "frivolity." She was a good, sturdy, suitable match. And Annie Pim was patient: "As I have learned to rough it, and may sometimes be a little rough myself," Cope admitted, "a very sensitive woman would trouble herself."

They married on August 15, 1865, and their only child, Julia, was born ten months later.

All seemed sober and settled. Cope had a warm home and a supportive family; he could now hunker down and work. He seemed to want stability above all else now, but it wasn't in Cope's nature to stay calm, cool, and collected for long. Annie's temperament may have allowed for a congenial home life; his colleagues wouldn't get off so easily.

The Professor

"I changed my mind during an afternoon spent on Dracut Heights. I resolved that I would return to Andover, take hold, and really study." —O. C. MARSH

M arsh took a very different path to prominence, one that would shape him as both a scientist and Cope's rival.

Born in 1831, nine years after the word "paleontology" came into use, Othniel (the boy hated his given name and more often went by "O. C.") knew humble beginnings. He was raised on a hardscrabble farm near Lockport, New York. His mother died young, as Edward Cope's had—when he was just three—but unlike the pampered Quaker, O. C. got little attention from his new stepmother. There were plenty of half siblings for her to see to, and he and his older sister, Mary, were left to their own devices. They became, in many ways, their own family—separate and inseparable.

While Mary nurtured O. C., their father, Caleb, had just one stern ambition

O. C. Marsh, 1865.

for him: the boy would earn his keep on the family farm. Caleb expected his son—who had "good natural abilities and some mechanical ingenuity"—to work, and work hard.

But just as Edward resisted "gentlemanly" farming, O. C. hated drudgery, evading chores at all costs and earning his father's wrath in the bargain. The boy had "a roving disposition," Caleb complained.

Rural New York was a far cry from Philadelphia, the nation's cultural and scientific center. There wasn't a world-class museum to escape to, and O. C. kept his own counsel and had few companions.

He did befriend a neighbor, a retired military colonel named Ezekiel Jewett, who was impressed with his shooting and let the boy tag along on hunting excursions. Jewett was also an amateur geologist, and with minerals and fossils plentiful along the banks of Lockport Canal, they might as easily flush those out as wildlife.

By age twenty-one, O. C. had had only a scattershot education. To escape the farm, he tried his hand at teaching in Millport, New York, but didn't take

WHERE DID THEY GO?

In the eighteenth century, the field of geology was already raising stubborn questions about the age of the earth (and undermining, by suggestion, the biblical framework of Creation). By the late 1700s, the French anatomist and zoologist Georges Cuvier was stepping up the pace of inquiry.

The dominant theory at the time was that fossils reflected animals still present somewhere on earth; the world was as it had always been, as God created it, fixed in time and space. That species could change or disappear for good was a shocking, even blasphemous idea, though fossil hunters were beginning to uncover traces of mysterious beasts—ichthyosaurs, plesiosaurs, pterodactyls—that had never been seen alive by anyone, anywhere.

Using comparative anatomy to reconstruct a vanished world, Cuvier offered evidence that the past was *unlike* the present. He proved that African and Indian elephants were distinct species, and that massive elephant-like remains unearthed in Europe and Siberia belonged

to life as a rural schoolmaster. He moved to Massachusetts to be near Mary (her husband, Robert, described his brother-in-law's character as "hardly formed and developed") and was stoking a faint ambition to try carpentry or surveying next when fate stepped in.

An inheritance from his mother's estate, managed by her millionaire brother, George Peabody, allowed O. C. to enroll in prestigious Andover Academy.

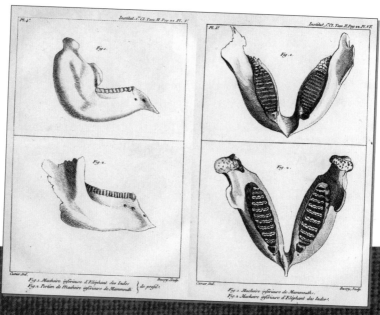

Cuvier's figure of the jaw of an Indian elephant and the fossil jaw of a mammoth, 1799.

to neither, but to an extinct giant known today as a woolly mammoth.

Cuvier identified American mastodons, giant ground sloths, Irish elk, and other vanished species—all evidence of a biological endgame. He also proposed that *mass* extinctions had occurred, triggered by geological "catastrophes," or jarring changes on the face of earth.

Once it was accepted that species died out, it was a matter of time before scientists began to ask how and why, allowing the study of the fossil past to become a formal scientific discipline in its own right, alongside anatomy and geology. Cuvier's methods were adopted by leading anatomists of the day, including Richard Owen, Joseph Leidy, Louis Agassiz, and, eventually, Marsh and Cope, and he is widely considered the "father of paleontology."

Set loose from the toil and ragged emotions of life on the farm, he reveled in his freedom. He made "little impression" academically that first year, often skipping class to play backgammon or roam out in search of minerals and fossils.

But the following summer, things changed. He changed.

Mary, who had married, died in childbirth. The loss of his beloved sister hit O. C. hard. While pacing along Dracut Heights one afternoon, he decided he needed to own his life. He would go back and give school another try, "take hold, and really study."

He discovered he had a knack for applying himself. He loved outthinking opponents and outdoing competitors, for one thing. O. C. studied nonstop but went out of his way to make it look easy, whether or not it was. He became a shrewd manager—"shrewd with a touch of cunning in it," recalled a classmate. He was steadfast and determined, and once he fixed his mind on a goal, there was no stopping him.

O. C. steadily rose to the top of his class, and stayed there. Impressed with his progress, his uncle, George Peabody, took charge of his nephew's education; he sent O. C. to Yale and picked up the tab (scolding him often for spending too much and keeping poor accounts).

As at Andover, O. C. was older than his Yale peers, who nicknamed him "Daddy" or "Captain." Though he had more acquaintances than friends, these praised his burly strength and outdoor skills. Marsh knew how to forge connections and make things run, skills that would serve him well in the field.

Science and geology soon commanded all his attention. He doted on his collections. Even as an undergraduate, he had a possessive streak, locking precious minerals and fossils in an attic room at his boarding house. At one point the collection loomed so large that his landlord, who kept rooms below, had to prop supports under the floor. The landlord's daughter recalled him trotting her upstairs on his shoulders to see the treasure—"Libby, if you promise not to touch, I'll show you some wonderful things." But his doors were resolutely closed to others, those he didn't trust. "He was always very odd," she explained, "and for most people it was like 'running against a pitchfork' to get acquainted with him."

On a trip to Canada in 1855, twenty-four-year-old O. C. found two interesting fossil vertebrae (backbone pieces) on cliffs at the Bay of Fundy. He thought they were a fish species, but he wasn't sure, so he set them aside to analyze down the line.

In 1860, Marsh graduated eighth in his class with a scholarship for graduate study at Yale's highly regarded Sheffield Scientific School, taking advanced classes in geology, chemistry, physics, and botany. He shared the Canadian fossil he'd found with his geology professor, who urged him to send it on to Harvard's Louis Agassiz.

A world expert on ancient fishes, and one of the nation's major scientists, Agassiz proposed that the fossil was an unknown extinct animal with both fish and amphibian traits. Marsh decided the great scientist was wrong and had the audacity to

Louis Agassiz, 1870.

FISHY FINDINGS

Swiss American biologist and geologist Louis Agassiz (1807–73), a student of Cuvier's, used his mentor's comparative anatomy methods to explore living and fossil fishes and the way glacial episodes alter species and landforms over time. He was the first scientist to propose the concept of an ice age, in 1837.

say so. He repossessed the specimen to look more closely on his own. The bones, he later asserted, were from an animal related to ancient sea reptiles, or ichthyosaurs. Marsh named his find *Eosaurus* ("early lizard") *acadianus* ("from Acadia").

In fall 1862, with graduate degree in hand, Marsh toured Europe to study paleontology at German universities. He also managed to convince George Peabody to pledge a small fortune to Yale University to fund a world-class natural history museum. The university repaid his uncle's "munificent donation" by awarding Marsh a professorship. The geology post was taken, so Yale devised a professorship of paleontology, the nation's first—a position Marsh held for more than thirty years (much of the time without salary, so he could spend his days collecting instead of teaching).

Marsh used that European tour as an opportunity to buy up fossils and books for his museum-in-progress, a heaping two and a half tons of them. He also called on important scientists, including the father of evolutionary theory, Charles Darwin himself, a profound influence on the younger scientist.

And, in Berlin, he met Edward Drinker Cope—the friend he would soon, whether he set out to or not, betray.

LIKE CONFESSING A MURDER

A year after the excavation of *Hadrosaurus foulkii* in America, a shy and reclusive naturalist across the Atlantic, a man "not apt to follow blindly the lead of other men," published a book that would change the course of science forever.

When geology first emerged as a discipline, the idea that landforms and life-forms had transformed over big swaths of time, and that our world might be much, much older than the human race, disturbed many people of European-Christian descent by undermining a literal reading of the Bible.

The revolutionary ideas in Charles Darwin's *On the Origin of Species*—that God had not created life on earth all at once, and that plants and animals evolved over time, descending from similar species of the distant past—so unnerved the author that he held back his research for twenty years.

During that time, Darwin quietly experimented and collected proof, drawing on his youthful voyage to South America aboard the HMS *Beagle*; on continuing observation of beetles, barnacles, and pigeons; and on the work of Georges Cuvier, geologists William Smith and Charles Lyell, and others. "It is like confessing a murder," he admitted, when he at last released his findings to the world.

The idea of evolution by natural selection, independently arrived at by the British biologist Alfred Russel Wallace—an important (if lesser-known) coauthor of the theory—rattled Victorian society to its core and had an enormous intellectual impact on Marsh, a senior at Yale when *On the Origin of Species* was published.

Marsh would be a Darwinian thinker all his life and contribute important findings to Darwin's theories, but in 1859, the theories were profoundly unsettling to much of society.

Charles Darwin, 1878.

3

A Theft

"I took him through New Jersey and showed him the localities. . . . Soon after . . . I found everything closed to me and pledged to Marsh for money." —E. D. COPE

I n 1866, the unveiling of the world's first standing dinosaur was still two years away. Benjamin Waterhouse Hawkins had yet to construct his masterpiece for the academy in Philadelphia, but nearby Haddonfield—where the fossil remains had been found—was already on the map, a focal point for the brave new science of dinosaur paleontology.

Once a Cretaceous seabed, the mud under much of southwestern New Jersey oozed mineral-dense marl or greensand, a rich organic blend of clay, sand, and limestone. For ages, ordinary folk had been digging up marl in the area to sell as fertilizer, turning over modest fossil bones, teeth, and shells in the process and ignoring them, mostly.

After the 1859 discovery of *Hadrosaurus*, the academy had publicly

Skeleton of Hadrosaurus as restored by Benjamin Waterhouse Hawkins, 1868.

lamented that "valuable illustrations of palaeontology and geology are annually lost through the ignorance of marl diggers or the inattention of owners of pits." It was a travesty that a region so rich in rarities and so near Philadelphia and the museum should go unmonitored. It was "important that measures . . . be taken to awaken in the minds of proprietors and workmen an interest in the preservation of specimens for the cabinet of the Academy."

They urged area pit operators to alert the museum to fossil finds, and informed hunters began actively combing the marl for skeletons. Cope took to the field himself, crossing the Delaware River in his free time to explore the muddy region north and south of Haddonfield.

Some local companies had agreed to alert the academy to finds, and in August 1866, J. C. Voorhees of the West Jersey Marl Company summoned Cope for a look at one.

"I thought best to go down at once," Cope wrote to his father.

He hired a carriage in Camden the next morning and was richly rewarded when he arrived on-site. "I found the remains of much greater interest than I had anticipated," he gushed, "being nothing more nor less than a totally new gigantic carnivorous dinosaurian."

FOULKE'S BULKY LIZARD

The story of the resurrected *Hadrosaurus* began in Haddonfield, New Jersey, on a farm owned by a financier, John Estaugh Hopkins, in 1838.

Like many wealthy nineteenth-century landowners in that agricultural part of the state, Hopkins harvested marl to sell as fertilizer. When diggers mining on his property unearthed giant fossilized vertebrae, Hopkins did what many in this faddish heyday of natural history collecting did: displayed them at his summer home. Visitors marveled, and other wealthy vacationers took to digging for treasure to fill their own "curiosity cabinets."

Twenty years passed before anyone thought to consider the fossils from the perspective of science, and by then, most or all of Hopkins's monstrous vertebrae had been carried off by enthusiastic visitors.

When the vacationing William Parker Foulke stopped by Hopkins's farm for

Cope's prize, including a rear leg, a jaw piece, and "a cross between the talon of an eagle and the claw of a lion," was wholly new to science, "probably of Buckland's genus *Megalosaurus*," he wrote to his father—his imagination for prehistory kicking into high gear—"which was the devourer and destroyer of Leidy's *Hadrosaurus*, and of all else it could lay claws on."

Cope eventually decided against the English genus *Megalosaurus* and named the creature *Laelaps* (after a mythical Greek hunting dog who always caught her quarry) *aquilunguis* ("terrible leaper with eagle claws"). *Laelaps* was, he told Alfred proudly, "altogether the finest discovery I have yet made."

He was twenty-six years old and had laid hands on the country's second major dinosaur discovery.

As would become his habit, Cope dashed off a scientific paper, one his friend Marsh would surely read, describing a ferocious, two-legged predator, roughly twenty feet long, that sprang at prey with fearsome "birdlike" claws.

dinner one summer night in 1858, his friend mentioned the strange bones. A Victorian gentleman lawyer and fossil hobbyist, Foulke was also a member of Philadelphia's prestigious Academy of Natural Sciences.

He had heard about the great prehistoric beasts called dinosaurs at academy meetings and grasped at once the significance of his friend's find.

Hopkins no longer had much of anything to show from the original excavation, but he could point Foulke to the site. It took some searching, but once the spot was located, Foulke got his friend's permission to hire a crew to try to unearth more bones from the slimy marl. They hit pay dirt with back and tail vertebrae, plus many fragments. Foulke called in fellow academy member Dr. Joseph Leidy, the nation's go-to expert on fossil life, who would describe the find for science.

GOD'S WHIMSY

The ancient Greeks suspected that fossils were the remains of long-dead organisms, and independent thinkers like Leonardo da Vinci (1452–1519) studied them. But until the nineteenth century, most human cultures explained fossils in mystical terms, as animals and plants turned to stone by magic, or as proof of giants and dragons. Some believed the beasts had died in the great biblical flood or that the shells and teeth that seemed to bloom inside the earth were ornamental gifts of God's whimsy—just as flowers were aboveground—or that they crystallized like gems.

While people wondered and speculated about the origins of their discoveries, before the 1840s fossils unearthed by accident rarely made their way to scientists; few scientists, for that matter, took the time to catalog prehistoric treasures. Most "collections" were informal or eccentric. Legend has it that one of the bones from the original *Hadrosaurus* excavation was put to work as an umbrella stand!

An eighteenth-century etching with fossil forms.

LIKE COPE, MARSH WAS VERY MUCH settled back in the United States by this point. He had taken up his post at Yale and was devoting all his time to work. (Unlike Cope, Marsh would never marry or have children.)

Newly wed Cope had a young family to care for; he had been appointed secretary at the academy; and he was teaching zoology at Haverford. But he was as restless a professor as he had been a student—and his argumentative nature had emerged again. "Flummery there is and will be at Haverford," he wrote his father. His days at the college were numbered.

In 1867, fresh off the thrill of

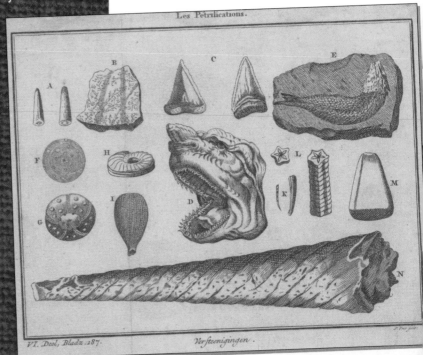

Les Petrifications.

VI. Deel, Bladz. 287.   Versteenigingen.

Leaping Laelaps, *by Charles R. Knight, 1897.*

discovering *Laelaps*, Cope resigned from teaching to devote himself to paleontology. He moved Annie and baby Julia to Haddonfield to be by the marl pits and lobbied his father for "something to spend on scientific work."

The same year, with his Marsh correspondence in full swing, Cope named one of his amphibian fossil finds *Ptyonius marshii* in his friend's honor.

NOT LONG AFTER *LAELAPS*, COPE WOULD BE PROMOTED TO CURATOR AT THE academy, laboring alongside Leidy to prepare *Hadrosaurus* for display, a project that had been much delayed by the Civil War and other factors.

As news of their work spread, scientists and museums throughout North America and Europe took notice.

Marsh took notice of the notice. In his role as America's first college professor of paleontology, he had been feverishly collecting dinosaur tracks in the Connecticut River Valley—feverishly collecting in general—and the marl-rich fields of southern New Jersey, as documented by Cope in his *Laelaps* article, were of profound interest. In 1868 he decided to visit.

Cope recorded the outing in a letter to his father. "After the work of the winter," he wrote, "I have been taking a little outdoor exercise as it has come conveniently in the shape of a trip through the Marl country. I had intended making it this season, but not so early. My friend, Prof. Marsh of Yale College, had however planned to go a little earlier, so I accompanied him."

Though his energy ran high, Cope was busy, unwell, and tired when Marsh arrived in his home territory that spring. But the pair set out to explore the muck for two weeks anyway.

A CRAZE FOR FERNS AND FOSSILS

Throughout most of the nineteenth century, the Victorians—people alive during the long reign of England's Queen Victoria—were wild about natural history. The growth of the middle classes in industrialized England and America meant more people had the time and leisure to explore and marvel at the world around them, and they did, in droves.

Museums and botanical gardens sprouted to educate and entertain this curious public and inform them of scientific discoveries. Enthusiasts gathered for evenings around microscopes, launched collecting clubs, and fanned out at the beach in search of exotic seaweed, drying and pasting their finds in scrapbooks. Books with names like *Marvels of Pond Life* became bestsellers, and clergymen praised the virtues of acquiring feathers and fungi.

Whether focused on rocks, ferns, shells, mushrooms, butterflies, beetles, or fish, acquisition mania abounded, and no middle-class drawing room was complete without stuffed birds, a drawer of gemstones, or a tank of exotic fish.

Most scientists at the time were amateurs, hobbyists who observed and recorded phenomena or amassed specimens to catalog and display in home curiosity cabinets. "Gentleman" and "lady" scientists traveled the world, drawing, describing, and collecting plants and animals.

Much of the fossil record was still scattered, but now and then an amateur find like Foulke's *Hadrosaurus* would electrify the scientific community.

The weather was often bad, leaving Cope under it in all respects, but they worked side by side, happily uncovering "three new species of Saurians."

Along the way, they met and rubbed elbows with a number of marl pit foremen and managers. Cope made these introductions—to the men who notified the academy when workmen struck bone, including Voorhees of the West Jersey Marl Company—in good faith. Why shouldn't he? What he didn't know was that his friend and competitor was having conversations out of earshot.

Marsh would circle back on the sly at some point and, in a feat of practical magic, open his wallet.

After that, workers no longer directed interesting bones to the academy in Philadelphia. All alerts would now go to Yale.

A painting of a cabinet of curiosities by Domenico Remps.

4

An "Abominable Volume" and a Hat Full of Bones

"My own life work seemed laid out before me."

—O. C. MARSH

A few months after his visit to Haddonfield, Professor Marsh boarded a train. It wasn't just any train; it was a Union Pacific steam engine bound for Benton, Wyoming, the end of the line—at the time—of a spanking-new transcontinental railroad. Tracks had been inching across the windswept Great Plains since 1863.

The ride, sponsored by Chicago's annual meeting of the American Association for the Advancement of Science, was a revelation.

While he was in school in Germany, Marsh had scribbled in a notebook, "The most inviting field for Paleontology in North America is in the unsettled regions of the west." English geologist Charles Lyell had been there before

A Union Pacific Railroad excursion to the hundredth meridian, 1866.

him, back in 1842, and declared, "Certainly in no other country are these ancient strata developed on a grander scale or more plentifully charged with fossils."

But since he got back from Europe, the only place besides Haddonfield where Marsh had done hands-on collecting was in the Connecticut River Valley. Fossils were hard to access east of the Mississippi.

The American West was, no question, the most fertile field in the United States, and now, from the comfort of a rattling coach, Marsh watched through the glass as a kaleidoscopic landscape, "new and strange," blurred by. To arrive "in the middle of these plains, stretching in every direction as far as the eye could see," was a sensation beyond any he could have imagined. He might spend a lifetime exploring here—and, in a way, he would.

One station stop Marsh hoped to make was at tiny Antelope Junction, Nebraska. According to news reports, locals had unearthed strange bones there while digging a well. They were "undoubtedly human," claimed one reporter. Other sources attributed the bones to a tiger or an elephant. Marsh smelled a humbug and felt called to investigate.

As they chuffed up to the station platform, he got the conductor to pause the train long enough for him to look in on the nearby dig site.

Beside the well, Marsh found a mound of earth. Sifting through dirt and sediment, he did indeed find bones and fragments. The mound was thick with them, but they weren't, he believed, human bones.

He snapped to when the conductor blew the whistle. As the train threatened to chug away, the professor struck a lightning-fast deal with a station agent, then leaped aboard the westbound caboose.

Nearing the Rockies later, the train scaled the bed of an ancient great freshwater lake. Marsh's mind churned over the possibilities. "I was eager to explore it," he recalled later, "sure that entombed in the sandy clays to the brim there must be hidden the remains of many strange animals new to science."

His optimism was tangibly rewarded on the trip back home. When his eastbound train puffed into Antelope Junction, the stationmaster was waiting.

As agreed, the man had collected the remaining bones from the mound, and he now handed the professor a "hat full of bones."

"I left in his palm glittering coin of the realm," Marsh wrote, recalling his elation, "and we parted good friends."

As the train continued east, he sorted his catch while other passengers crowded round to watch. "I showed them to my fellow travelers. . . . Recalling the old adage that 'truth lies at the bottom of a well,' I

ON

THE ORIGIN OF SPECIES

BY MEANS OF NATURAL SELECTION,

OR THE

PRESERVATION OF FAVOURED RACES IN THE STRUGGLE FOR LIFE.

BY CHARLES DARWIN, M.A.,

FELLOW OF THE ROYAL, GEOLOGICAL, LINNÆAN, ETC., SOCIETIES; AUTHOR OF 'JOURNAL OF RESEARCHES DURING H. M. S. BEAGLE'S VOYAGE ROUND THE WORLD.'

LONDON:
JOHN MURRAY, ALBEMARLE STREET.
1859.

The right of Translation is reserved.

The 1859 title page of Charles Darwin's "abominable volume."

MISSING PROOF

On the Origin of Species was an instant bestseller when it came out, and caused a storm of controversy on both sides of the Atlantic. Supporters hoped paleontology might offer hard evidence in support of the theories in Darwin's self-proclaimed "abominable volume."

Though a few rare finds had connected some of the dots, the still-young study of

it answered. There were glaring absences in the fossil record, and even Darwin had to wonder: Were dinosaurs just massive extinct creatures with no relation to the animal forms that came before or after? Or were they truly part of a continuum?

Proof lay in these missing "transitional" forms, but were they needles in a vast geologic haystack?

could only wonder, if such scientific truths as I had now obtained were concealed in a single well, what untold treasure must be in the whole Rocky Mountain region. This thought promised rich rewards for the enthusiastic explorer in this new field."

The fossil bounty marked some eleven species of extinct reptiles and mammals, including an ancient turtle, camel, and pig. But what riveted Marsh were the bones of a little horse.

"During his life he was scarcely a yard in height," he wrote, describing the creature he would name *Equus parvulus* ("little horse," today known as *Protohippus parvulus*), and "each of his slender legs was terminated by three toes."

SHE SELLS SEASHELLS BY THE SEASHORE

Though she was the inspiration for this famous tongue twister, Mary Anning didn't set out to be a renowned fossil hunter and geologist.

Two hundred million years ago, what is now Lyme Regis—the seaside town in West Dorset, England, where Anning lived—was underwater and teeming with life. By her era, exposed marine beds up and down the coast revealed the remains of marvelous creatures.

Mary was born in 1799 into extreme poverty. Her parents had nine children, though only she and her brother Joseph would survive to adulthood, and her father, who kept a beach stall to sell souvenirs to tourists, often took the family out scouring the shore for shells and stone "sea lilies." Mary had a special knack for the work, and after her father fell from a cliff and died in 1810, leaving the family in dire financial straits, her skills helped them survive.

Day after day Mary went out with her dog, Tray, to comb the cliffs, especially in winter, when storms hammered the coastline and landslides made it easy to spot fossils (though recovering them in bitter winds before they—or she and her dog!—were seized by the tide was anything but). It was dangerous work, and she nearly perished in an 1833 landslide that killed Tray.

In 1811, when she was twelve, Mary

Mary Anning with her dog, Tray, painted before 1842.

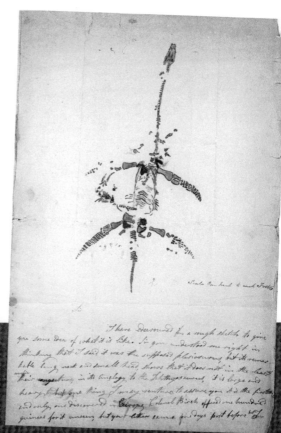

Letter and drawing from Mary Anning announcing the discovery of a fossil animal now known as Plesiosaurus dolichodeirus, *December 1823.*

and Joseph unearthed the first complete fossil *Ichthyosaurus*, a marine reptile with flippers. This and other remarkable discoveries found homes in museums, academies, and the cabinets of rich private collectors—and an astonishing, near-complete sea reptile uncovered in 1823 would make her famous: her long-necked *Plesiosaurus* baffled even Georges Cuvier. (It was too fabulous to be true: the neck alone had some thirty-five vertebrae!)

In time, Cuvier pronounced Anning's fossil genuine, and Darwin took it as proof that prehistoric life was nothing like life in the present.

Working class, female, self-taught

(at a time when women weren't allowed to attend university or advance in the sciences), unmarried, and solitary, Mary Anning stood boldly apart in a field dominated by London gentlemen.

Because she rarely wrote out or formally published her findings, others took scientific credit for her discoveries. But in 2010—163 years after her death—London's prestigious Royal Society named her one of ten British women who most influenced the history of science.

An enthusiastic supporter of Darwin's theories, Marsh had scored an ancestor of modern horses! *Equus parvulus* was a link in a chain leading from the little three-toed model up to the present-day horse.

What other links might be hidden out there in the plains and lake beds and buttes? Could the West, in time, provide hard evidence, a picture of evolution in action?

To a paleontologist and follower of Darwin, the West showed staggering promise, and Marsh couldn't wait to dig in—literally—but wait he would. Unrest among Sioux and Cheyenne made an excursion that year out of the question.

Consolation came in the form of a crate shipped by none other than J. C. Voorhees of the West Jersey Marl Company. It was waiting when Marsh returned to Yale, and inside were the ancient bones of an enormous marine reptile.

Marsh analyzed the fossil and took the opportunity to return Cope's favor of the year before—or twist the knife, perhaps—by naming his find after the Philadelphian.

Marsh's "new and gigantic serpent" from New Jersey would be known to science as *Mosasaurus* ("Meuse lizard"—the first was found near the Meuse River) *copeanus* (named for Cope).

Tough negotiating, sliding loyalties, and even double crosses were common in the rough-and-tumble world of fossil hunting—and Marsh's rustic upbringing may have given him the advantage over Cope here.

In no way flattered, Cope took to calling his namesake fossil "the one that got away."

It was a while before news of Marsh's duplicitous arrangement with Voorhees trickled down to him, but when it did, Cope would remember it as the beginning of the end of their friendship.

5

A Mistake

> *"[Cope's] wounded vanity received a shock from
> which it has never recovered, and he has since been
> my bitter enemy."*
>
> —O. C. MARSH

Marsh remembered the beginning of the end quite differently.

The Yale professor wasn't the only one to receive a significant parcel in 1868.

However stung Cope might have been by his friend's underhandedness, he didn't dwell on it; in March, an exciting distraction arrived at the academy. A field agent at Fort Wallace, Kansas, had sent several crates packed with the fossil bones of a massive Cretaceous marine reptile. Like Marsh's mosasaur, it had inhabited the shallow ocean that once covered central North America, but the creature Cope identified as a plesiosaur was not only bigger than Marsh's specimen; it was the most complete skeleton of its kind that Cope had ever seen.

Cardiff Giant, 1869.

He set to cleaning and reassembling. His agent had shipped more than a hundred bones—vertebrae, hip, shoulder, limbs, and a precious skull—all swaddled in old newspaper, bound in burlap, and nestled in the crates.

Gingerly, Cope unwound each piece, chipping away clay crust to get to bone. He sorted the bones, reconnecting them as Leidy had taught him, using comparative methods developed by Cuvier.

When at last, a full year later, Cope had unpuzzled and rebuilt the animal, the skeleton spanned thirty-five feet. It had giant fins attached to platelike hip and chest bones, an angular head with pointy teeth, and what appeared to be a strangely flexible neck.

Cope named his sea monster *Elasmosaurus platyurus*, ("Flat-tailed plate-reptile") and proposed a whole new taxonomic order—Streptosauria ("twisted reptiles")—to classify its unique magnificence.

His major scientific paper, printed with illustrated plates at his own expense, would circulate with the transactions of the American Philosophical Society later that year and be read by other important paleontologists, including Marsh.

Both men were on a roll and eager for the other to know it.

With the threat of Indian-Army violence still looming in the West, Marsh put off staging an expedition and planned a trip east to Philadelphia to see Benjamin Waterhouse Hawkins's acclaimed *Hadrosaurus foulkii*.

He made a stop, too, that fall in Syracuse, New York, to investigate a proposed miracle.

Thousands had already paid their fifty cents to enter the pavilion and view the wonder—a giant, petrified man the press had christened the Cardiff Giant—including Oliver Wendell Holmes, Ralph Waldo Emerson, and other prominent thinkers.

As it happened, Marsh would gleefully pull the rug out from under the phenomenon. The figure unearthed on a farm in the rural village of Cardiff, New York, however impressive to the untrained eye, was no ancient Phoenician relic but a recent plant "well calculated to impose upon the general public." The figure was carved of water-soluble gypsum, Marsh pointed out, yet still bore tool marks. The "ancient" giant was a modern hoax, designed to fool and belittle the masses and turn a buck (or a great many bucks). What amazed him was that other scientists had fallen for the ruse. It was one thing to fool

"I found myself as if placed in a charnel house . . . surrounded by mutilated fragments of many hundred skeletons of more than twenty kinds of animals, piled confusedly around me. The task assigned me was to restore them all to their original positions. . . . [With] comparative anatomy every bone and fragment of a bone resumed its place."

—Georges Cuvier

READING THE BONES

Fossil organisms are related to living animals. Anatomical and skeletal forms are similar across species: skulls attach to backbones, legs to hips, and so on. With very few bones, then—and proportions in mind—the comparative anatomist can reconstruct and identify any creature. (Cuvier, for example, boasted he could name a species with only one bone!)

When Joseph Leidy described *Hadrosaurus foulkii*, he determined it was a near relative of the *Iguanodon* discovered decades earlier in England. He wasn't one to theorize, but given the creature's short arm bones and much

longer leg bones, Leidy drew a startling conclusion in his address to the academy: that *Hadrosaurus* may have reared back on hind legs like a kangaroo.

At a time when scientists believed that dinosaurs crawled on all fours like modern reptiles, the idea of a bipedal dinosaur was exciting, hinting at a diverse range of giants that might as easily stride upright on two legs as scramble across prehistoric earth on all fours.

Portrait of Georges Cuvier by François-André Vincent, 1795.

the general public, but geologists should know better, and many didn't; at least two prominent earth scientists had publicly miscalculated the giant's age. It was laughable and, for some, embarrassing.

When word reached Cope that Marsh would pay a visit to the academy, he must have rejoiced at the timing. Almost overnight, Philadelphia's formerly sleepy museum had become a bustling destination, thanks to Hawkins's masterpiece, and Cope would have been happy to show off accomplishments past and present. Here was his opportunity

Benjamin Waterhouse Hawkins, 1875.

THE JOLLY OLD BEAST IS NOT DECEASED

Philadelphia's *Hadrosaurus* wasn't Hawkins's first public success. The artist had already received acclaim as the creator, with help from scientist Richard Owen, of the world's first public dinosaur display on the grounds of London's Crystal Palace. Queen Victoria supported his efforts, but Hawkins was an educator as well as an artist and wanted approval from England's scientific elite, too; so he set out to woo them with style. He handcrafted twenty-one invitations to an exclusive New Year's Eve party. He had his iguanodon mold transported outdoors, built a platform with steps, and raised a huge tent over his surprise.

On December 31, 1853, Hawkins

and top hat to unveil his masterpiece at what would be the scientific event of that or any season.

For eight hours, footmen scurried back and forth, up and down platform steps, carrying silver platters of pigeon pie, ham, rabbit, fish, pastry, plums, and pudding. Inside the beast's belly, an elite group of scientists and supporters celebrated Hawkins's project with merry shouting and speeches. By midnight, the party was toasting Hawkins, the occasion, and the iguanodon with a commemorative song:

The jolly old beast
Is not deceased
There's life in him again!

to one-up the man who had "stolen" *Mosasaurus* out from under him on his own turf.

Marsh arrived eager to see what his competitors were up to, and Cope escorted him behind the scenes for a peek at his new prize. It's easy to imagine Marsh circling the great skeleton of *Elasmosaurus*, hands behind his back, shrewd, close-set blue eyes fixed on his rival's effort. It's just as easy to imagine his pompous delight as he stroked his beard and squinted down at Cope's staggering mistake.

"I noticed that the articulations of the vertebrae were reversed," he recalled years later, pointing out ("gently," he maintained) that Cope "had the whole thing wrong end foremost."

Cope had put the beast's skull on its tail.

Impossible! Cope had devoted an entire year to painstaking study of the bones.

As Marsh later recalled, "His indignation was great, and he asserted in strong language that he had studied the animal for many months and ought at least to know one end from another."

According to legend, the men wrangled and sniped, and the debate grew heated. Mild-mannered Dr. Leidy—an old-school gentleman, no doubt wincing all the while—was called in to settle the score. Unlike Marsh, Leidy wasn't the type to gloat when a fellow scientist was on the hot seat, especially a colleague like Cope, who had trained with him. But facts were facts.

Benjamin Waterhouse Hawkins's account of the Crystal Palace dinner held in 1853.

SCIENCE OR SIDESHOW?

Before O. C. Marsh exposed the Cardiff Giant, the great showman P. T. Barnum tried and failed to rent and exhibit the curiosity. He had a huge plaster re-creation of the giant made and put his own "True Goliath" on display at Wood's Museum, where the public paid to see it even after Marsh disproved the original.

Why line up and buy tickets to view a fraud, a humbug?

Still a new term in the mid-nineteenth century, "science" had a long-running association in America with show business. From freak shows and dime museums to traveling medicine men using theatrics and song to pitch bottled potions, popular entertainment often tempered the sensational with "science." Newspaper headlines called out discoveries later disproved as hoaxes: Life on the moon! Petrified babies! Man-eating trees! Fairies on film!

Barnum's beloved American Museum in New York exposed the public to real exotic wildlife right alongside humbugs like his infamous dried "Feejee mermaid." The showman who would later promote "The Greatest Show on Earth" knew better than anyone how to appeal to human curiosity. He understood that people were willing to be fooled if they enjoyed themselves in the process. But the hoaxes and "quackery" of the era robbed real science and scientists of credibility.

Without a word, Leidy reversed the ends, fitting the skull snugly in place.

Cope was humiliated.

To save his reputation, he scrambled to call back every copy of the *Elasmosaurus* paper, but this was no easy feat, and Marsh and Leidy held on to theirs.

Questions of credibility in science were much in the news at the time, with legitimate scientists anxious to build systems and standards into their disciplines. Shoddy work

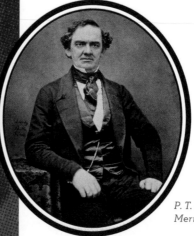

P. T. Barnum's Feejee Mermaid, 1842.

P. T. Barnum, 1850.

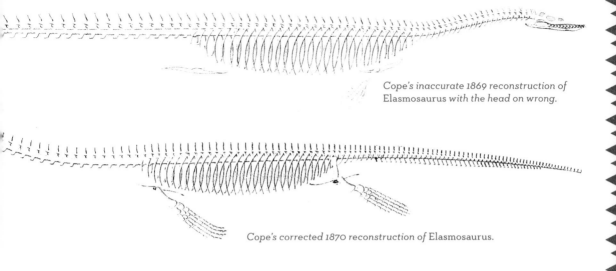

Cope's inaccurate 1869 reconstruction of Elasmosaurus with the head on wrong.

Cope's corrected 1870 reconstruction of Elasmosaurus.

reflected on everyone, and if science was going to be taken seriously by the public and receive funding, it was the task of all to hold each other accountable and present a dignified front.

At the March 8, 1870, meeting of the academy, Leidy formally corrected Cope's blunder, admitting that it was a natural mistake, based on an earlier error of his own. Leidy was as gracious and diplomatic as ever, intending only to set the scientific record straight. But the damage was done.

Recent findings suggest that Cope was more upset by Leidy's public exposure than Marsh's private sport, though Marsh claimed it made him Cope's "bitter enemy." Their association certainly didn't end with his piracy in Haddonfield or Cope's *Elasmosaurus* blunder. Throughout the 1860s, their correspondence makes light reference to both. Cope stayed in Haddonfield near the marl fields for seven years after Marsh supposedly froze him out of the area fossil market, which hints that spoils were still plentiful, and Cope may not have been as embarrassed by his gaffe as some sources claim. Such mistakes were not unusual in the fast-paced game of naming and describing extinct species. Paleontologists often had little hard evidence to base their assertions on and were obliged to revise them if and whenever necessary.

"[I] retained friendly relations with him," Marsh later admitted, "although at times [Cope's] eccentricity of conduct, to use no stronger term, was hard to bear."

The end for these two, it turns out, was just the beginning, and with his friend and rival humbled, Marsh turned his attentions west again.

Dinosaur specimens in America were still a rarity. The first reported find, fossil teeth from Montana, was in 1854. Leidy had described *Hadrosaurus* as recently as 1857. The pace picked up a bit from there—but Cope had made a concise list of American discoveries as of 1869, citing just eighteen dinosaur species from thirteen genera.

But if the promise Marsh sensed on his Union Pacific outing held, scarcity of fossils would soon be a thing of the past, and his collection for the Peabody Museum would flourish.

The question was, who would get there first?

ALL THIS THING CALLED SCIENCE

The image of the wild-eyed, visionary, bumbling scientist was a holdover from the days when alchemists (the closest historical parallel) were seen as sorcerers or eccentrics. An expansive young country like America had no tolerance for Old World magic and superstition.

Science was already challenging the public with staggering ideas: that the earth hadn't been created by God in seven days, as ordained in the Bible, but by geological forces over millions of years; that humans had evolved from apes; that messages could travel on electric wires across an ocean.

Dinosaurs must have seemed as incredible to most people as dragons or giants, and therefore as easy to dismiss as real.

The average American looked on scientific progress with skepticism and impatience. After the Civil War, growth, industry, and immigration were the topics of note. "I am tired of all this thing called science," one senator complained at an 1861 Smithsonian appropriations hearing. "What do we care about stuffed snakes, alligators, and all such things?"

You didn't need formal training to be an "expert" in the 1800s. Many scientists were self-taught, often doctors pursuing science in their free time. A mistake like Cope's would have been common, especially in a field as young as paleontology, which pieced together prehistoric puzzles on scant evidence. But to combat public suspicion, professionals seeking respect, advancement, and funding were calling for standards and accountability.

In toppling the Cardiff Giant, Marsh came off in the press as a new breed of scientist: university trained (on both sides of the Atlantic), a Yale graduate, a no-nonsense academic equipped to explain the impossible beasts buried under the feet of an expanding nation.

This notoriety, as Marsh arrived in Philadelphia and trained his meticulous eye on *Elasmosaurus*, was salt to Cope's wound.

O. C. Marsh, circa 1880.

THE YALE COLLEGE EXPEDITION OF 1870.

CHAPTER

6

This Country of Big Things

"As night closed over our geologists, cut off from civilization . . . they felt 'in for' something more than science."
—C. W. BETTS, *HARPER'S NEW MONTHLY MAGAZINE*

In spring 1870, Marsh organized an expedition to parts of Nebraska, Kansas, Colorado, Wyoming, and Utah.

His philanthropist uncle, George Peabody, had died, leaving him more than enough money to fund a fossil outing and ease his responsibilities at Yale (plus build a big, elegant house in which to go on amassing—and guarding—his vast collections of fossils and artifacts).

On June 30, 1870, Marsh and eleven Yale students—all volunteers from families rich enough to sponsor them—boarded a train in New Haven for North Platte in western Nebraska.

After outfitting themselves in Omaha, the rough-and-ready crew of scholars arrived at Nebraska's Fort McPherson bearing Marsh's letter of

Illustration from "The Yale College Expedition of 1870" in
Harper's New Monthly Magazine, *1871.*

introduction from William Sherman, commanding general of the US Army.

Unlike the hotheaded Cope, Professor Marsh understood strategy and enjoyed politics; his social connections would ease his way to and through the West.

The Yale College Expedition of 1870.

With few, if any, roads on the plains in those days, and train tracks only lately linking east to west, the expedition journeyed by rail to military forts, where it picked up transport and provisions, an army escort, and local guides.

The army offered practical support as well as protection from Sioux and Cheyenne enraged by ongoing government exploitation and slaughter. The Sioux especially were said to be "in a state of unusual excitement" when the team arrived. Native tribes would in no way welcome encroaching white treasure-seekers to their territories now, scientific or otherwise, and fear of attack proved "a matter of hourly apprehension."

The team made camp near the fort and ventured out "mounted on Indian ponies, and armed with rifle, revolver, geological hammer, and bowie-knife."

The major in command and Pawnee guides rode ahead, with the Pawnee scaling high bluffs and parting the grass to peer through, in search of hostile forces, and the expedition and troops followed along with wagons bulging with gear.

ANOTHER KIND OF RACE

Tens of thousands of workers, 80 percent of them Chinese American, labored for more than six years—in punishing heat, snowdrifts, and plagues of grasshoppers—to blast the tunnels, build the bridges, and lay track for a transcontinental railroad that would irrevocably "open up" the West.

In a breakneck race, the Central Pacific laid track eastward while the Union Pacific moved west. When the steel rails met, opening a floodgate for European settlers, the changes would be staggering. Life for millions of Native Americans who called the Great Plains home in the 1800s—Sioux, Arapaho, Comanche, Cheyenne, Pawnee, Paiute, Iowa, and other nations—would become a bitter struggle for survival. Though these tribes had fought off incursion for generations, bloody conflict, legal battles, and forced removal from sacred lands would ultimately destroy the Plains Indians' way of life.

1869. **May 10th.** 1869.
GREAT EVENT
Rail Road from the Atlantic to the Pacific
GRAND OPENING
—OF THE—
Union Pacific
RAIL ROAD,
PLATTE VALLEY ROUTE.
PASSENGER TRAINS LEAVE
OMAHA
ON THE ARRIVAL OF TRAINS FROM THE EAST.
THROUGH TO SAN FRANCISCO
In less than Four Days, avoiding the Dangers of the Sea!
Travelers for Pleasure, Health or Business
Will find a Trip over The New or Mountains Healthy and Pleasant.
LUXURIOUS CARS & EATING HOUSES
ON THE UNION PACIFIC RAIL ROAD.
PULLMAN'S PALACE SLEEPING CARS
RUN WITH ALL THROUGH PASSENGER TRAINS.
GOLD, SILVER AND OTHER MINERS!
Now is the time to seek your Fortunes in Nebraska, Wyoming, Arizona, Washington, Dakotah Colorado, Utah, Oregon, Montana, New Mexico, Idaho, Nevada or California.
CONNECTIONS MADE AT
CHEYENNE for DENVER, CENTRAL CITY & SANTA FE
AT OGDEN AND CORINNE FOR HELENA, BOISE CITY VIRGINIA CITY, SALT LAKE CITY AND ARIZONA
THROUGH TICKETS FOR SALE AT ALL PRINCIPAL RAILROAD OFFICES!
Be Sure they Read via Platte Valley or Omaha
Company's Office 72 La Salle St., opposite City Hall and Court House Square, Chicago.
CHARLES E. NICHOLS, Ticket Agent.
G. P. GILMAN,   JOHN P. HART,   J. BUDD,   W. SNYDER.

Union Pacific poster announcing the opening of the Transcontinental Railroad, 1869.

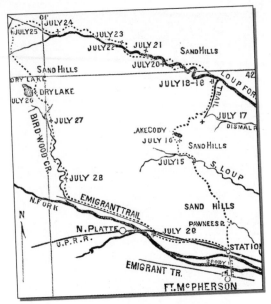

<image refr / (figure labels within map): OP JULY 24, JULY 25, JULY 23, JULY 22, JULY 21, SAND HILLS, JULY 20, DRY LAKE, DRY LAKE, JULY 26, JULY 18-19, LOUP FOR, TRAIL, 42, JULY 27, JULY 17, DISMAL R, BIRDWOOD CR., LAKE CODY, JULY 16, SAND HILLS, JULY 15, S. LOUP, JULY 28, EMIGRANT TRAIL, N. FORK, SAND HILLS, N. PLATTE, JULY 20, PAWNEES R., STATION, U.P.R.R., CODY, EMIGRANT TR., FT. McPHERSON, N />

Map illustration from "The Yale College Expedition of 1870" in Harper's New Monthly Magazine, 1871.

Conditions in the desert of sand hills between the Platte River and Loup Fork were grim. For two weeks Marsh and his team traversed dry, largely treeless plains under a burning sun. Some days, the thermometer soared to more than a hundred degrees in the shade, and the only shade was under the wagons. Until they reached Loup Fork, for fresh water, they "had to thank a thunder-shower," which allowed them to drink from the "rims of each other's hats."

"After fourteen hours in the saddle," one student wrote later, "one of the soldiers . . . finally exclaimed, 'What *did* God Almighty make such a country as this for?'" The country was "good enough," another quipped; it was the professor's "deuced geology" that "spoiled it all!"

Ribbing aside, Marsh was in his element in this harsh landscape among soldiers and frontiersmen. Known as "an outdoor man . . . a crack shot, a fisherman of repute, a seasoned camper," he was "at his best around a campfire where the swapping of tall tales is a highly appreciated art." Marsh could as easily hold his own with rough company as lecture his soldier escorts from the saddle on the "mighty changes of geology" that had formed the strange scenery all around them.

Their Fort McPherson entourage included, for a day (he was soon called away on other business), the famous frontier scout Buffalo Bill Cody, who joked around the campfire that first night, "The professor told the boys some mighty yarns to-day; but he tipped me a wink, as much as to say, 'you know how it is yourself, Bill!'"

Another member of the party recalled sitting in the glow of a bivouac fire "as night closed over our geologists, cut off from civilization," and his sense that they were "'in for' something more than science."

By day, as they traversed burning sand hills, Marsh would pause when something in the rocky passing bluffs caught his eye; if a site piqued his interest, he waved the students down from their mounts, they unpacked their tools, and the team set to work.

Over the next two weeks, the group uncovered the fossils of ancient camels, rhinoceroses, and horses that once

Buffalo Bill Cody, circa 1880.

roamed the plains. At night they pitched camp and sometimes saw mirroring columns of distant smoke or the glow of fires lit by Sioux hunting parties.

One prairie fire spread so close, they had to beat out falling sparks with blankets until a lucky thunderstorm intervened. The wind shifted the blaze away from their camp, but in the morning, they crossed "burned prairie that stretched on every side as far as the eye could reach, studded with roasted cactus and dead grasshoppers."

Illustration of a prairie fire from "The Yale College Expedition of 1870" in Harper's New Monthly Magazine, 1871.

Back at McPherson, the men crated up fossils and shipped their bounty east to New Haven by rail.

They put themselves on a westbound train for Cheyenne, Wyoming, fetching wagons, supplies, and thirty members of the Fifth Cavalry as escort from nearby Fort D. A. Russell.

Throughout August, Marsh and his crew circled through the West, collecting fossil turtles, birds, oreodonts (sheeplike plant eaters), brontotheres (rhino-like plant eaters), and a great many more. They forded rivers and braved narrow mountain passes on pack mules. They met a posse on the hunt for horse thieves and a company of "old-time trappers clad in buckskin" and weathered heat, thirst, and fatigue. There were buffalo runs, at least one run-in with a grizzly bear, and rattlesnakes—so many snakes that one romantic student shot enough to make a necklace of their rattles "for his lady-love."

In western Nebraska, Marsh led the party back to Antelope Junction,

WHERE THE BUFFALO ROAMED

In letters home to his family, Cope described his first "wonderful" glimpse of the Great Plains from the window of a Kansas Pacific railroad coach. There were prairies "more like ocean" and a herd of wild buffalo: "[O]nly 30 or 40 and the bulls tried to cross ahead of the engine," he reported with the same boyish glee he displayed in his childhood accounts of museum visits, "but became alarmed and turned back. They cantered along close to the cars, a splendid sight."

Cope told how there were "countless thousands" of buffalo around the fort, "millions they say between here and Denver." But he also described passengers firing their pistols at random, an exercise that left "carcasses and bones [lying] on each side of the R.R. track" for miles.

The great herds of North American buffalo were intricately bound to the Plains Indians and their way of life. Most tribes built their culture, community, and life cycle around the animals, depending on them for food, clothing, tools, and shelter. As late as the middle of the nineteenth century, tens of millions of wild buffalo still roamed the plains

"Father! Listen well. Your young men have gone on the path and have . . . killed my game and my buffalo. They did not kill them to eat; they left them to rot where they fell. Father, were I to go to your country to kill your cattle, what would you say? . . . Father, you talk about farming . . . I was raised on buffalo. . . . I was raised like your chiefs . . . to move my camps when necessary, to roam over the prairie at will. Take pity upon us; I am tired of talking."

—Chief Bear's Tooth

A pile of bison skulls, circa 1870.

(though they were already in decline). A single herd might span twenty-five miles.

But to the men building the continental railroad, the shaggy giants were little more than pests to be killed on sight, en masse. Their bulk blocked the rails, damaged track, and endangered passengers. The millions of white settlers and ranchers who later came west to farm the land agreed: the wild herds took up space, threatened resources, and were good only for sport hunting. They checked progress.

With hopes that the disappearing buffalo would return, tribes set mountain forests alight to clear more prairie. "Day after day," wrote one Marsh expedition member, "we saw heavy clouds of smoke rising, and night after night the mountainsides were masses of flames."

But the ongoing massacre would drive the animal to the edge of extinction. "Have the white men become children," demanded one Kiowa chief, "that they should kill meat and not eat?"

where he had stopped on his first train trip west. Marsh was overjoyed to find, near the well site, the bones of three more prehistoric horse species.

Illustration of a rattlesnake incursion from "The Yale College Expedition of 1870" in Harper's New Monthly Magazine, *1871.*

After establishing themselves at Fort Bridger in western Wyoming, the men struck out in search of the mythical junction of Utah's Green and White Rivers. Indians and travelers had long claimed that the Uinta Badlands, with their stark, chiseled buttes, gray clay, and bright cinnamon bluffs, were carpeted with monstrous bones.

They exited a mountain pass and stopped short at "the brink of a vast basin so desolate, wild, and broken, so lifeless and silent, that it seemed like the ruins of the world."

The last stretch of the journey brought them to western Kansas. Fierce winds pummeled them as they labored, combing the chalky Cretaceous rocks along Smoky Hill River, home of Cope's *Elasmosaurus*. Marsh had a mind to unearth his own sea serpent that November, one to rival his rival's, but his team found only a modest (by Wild West standards, which—along with the stakes and the egos involved—were expanding by the day) fifteen-foot mosasaur.

One evening, to avoid whistling gales, the team pitched camp below a tall rock bank. In the still of night, a coyote made brave by the smell of roasted buffalo leaped down into the cordon of pack animals, triggering panic in the camp. Everyone woke on high alert, but in the pitch-black chaos a number of terrified mules managed to kick loose and retreat. The men ruled out an Indian attack and shrugged off the missing mules; they needed daylight to track them, so they went back to bed.

When a dozen mules thundered into Fort Wallace the next morning, their eyes wild and their halters snapped, officers assumed the Cheyenne had attacked the professor's entourage, and they dispatched rescue. When the soldiers galloped up, they looked "more disappointed at losing the expected fight," one student recalled, "than gratified at our safety."

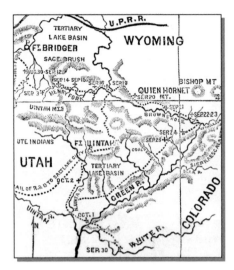

Map illustration from "The Yale College Expedition of 1870" in Harper's New Monthly Magazine, 1871.

WITH A CRUEL PLAINS WINTER AND THE THREAT OF SNOW LOOMING, THE expedition prepared to head east again.

Their adventure had come to an end, but on their last day in the field, Marsh spotted a mysterious small bone. As long as his palm and hollow like a bird's, the fossil had a distinctly un-birdlike joint at one end. He collected the form, intrigued, and marked the spot so he could return to dig further.

Tourists in the plush palace car of the Union Pacific coach sniffed as the motley crew of paleontologists clambered aboard.

The spanking-new buckskin breeches and army shirts purchased by fresh-faced scholars in Omaha were rank now. With duds worn and torn, their sun-browned faces bearing the "untrimmed stubble of a season," and an "open display of revolver and bowie-knife," the party had "a wild and warlike character" that set other passengers on edge.

MARSH'S TEAM RETURNED TO NEW HAVEN IN DECEMBER AFTER "SIX EVENTFUL months, during which [remarkably] no serious illness or accident" had plagued them.

Almost at once, the academic press began to hail the exploding "market for fossil vertebrates" in the West and Professor Marsh as the "most active figure in that market."

Thirty-six crates of fossils were waiting for him back at Yale. Marsh labored on their contents for months and began publishing papers on the bigger finds in early 1871.

The birdlike bone—from the wing of a pterodactyl, as it happened, a flying Cretaceous reptile—turned out to be big news all around.

Marsh "made a careful calculation of how large a Pterodactyl must be to have a wing finger" to match his fragment. "[I]ts spread of wings would be about twenty feet," he boasted, "truly a gigantic dragon even in this country of big things."

Scientists around the nation applauded the professor's accomplishments, and mainstream newspapers joined the fray. The public loved a good Wild West yarn, and the exploits of the Yale bone hunters—daily exposed to perils and privations—were sensational stuff. Two student participants published firsthand accounts, one in the popular *Harper's* magazine, and the attention can only have aggravated Cope's blocked ambitions and fed his envy.

Without Marsh's money, how could he compete?

In early July 1871, Marsh exacerbated things by circling back to Fort Wallace, Kansas, with yet another team of Yale students. The expedition raised camp along the Smoky Hill River, where he had found his first dragon bone. Marsh wanted the whole of that vast winged beast, and he found it, and several more pterodactyl skeletons besides.

A Pteranodon (a winged reptile of the order popularly called pterodactyl), described by O. C. Marsh, circa 1876.

In late August the expedition moved to Wyoming and dedicated six weeks to scouring Bridger Basin.

Here Marsh found rock from the geological epoch known as the Eocene jutting out of chalky hillsides or in plain view on the ground. It yielded a fossil bounty of ancient mammals: rhinoceroses, tapirs, and two more species of horse for his collection.

Possessive by nature, Marsh no doubt believed the Bridger and its bounty belonged to him, but back in Philadelphia, Cope was itching to prove him wrong.

7

Hi Toned for a Bone Sharp

> *"You will see therefore that while it is not a pleasant thing to work in competition with others it seems almost a necessity."*
>
> —FERDINAND VANDEVEER HAYDEN, GEOLOGIST AND SURVEY LEADER

Cope couldn't boast money. His wealthy but disappointed father measured the flow of family income, rarely funding his son's scientific endeavors, and unlike Marsh, Cope had no connections to arrange military escort.

He was a gentleman scientist without means, stuck far from the action.

Cope's mentor and boss at the academy already had a dependable flow of specimens coming in, many from Ferdinand Vandeveer Hayden, a geologist in charge of one of the big government surveys happening in the West; Leidy had no need or desire to do fieldwork himself.

Hayden's exploration of the high plains had won the academy many key

Edward Drinker Cope, 1895.

specimens. What if Cope went straight to Hayden for a job? It could be his ticket west.

Hoping his experience and association with Leidy would help him land a spot on Hayden's survey, Cope applied, but by summer he'd had no word.

Stuck in steamy Philadelphia cataloging and describing fossils sent by Leidy's suppliers, Cope grew more and more restless and impatient.

When news of Marsh's second Yale expedition reached him, he decided to brave western Kansas at his own expense. Cope couldn't sit on his hands any longer.

Arriving at Fort Wallace in early September, Cope secured a wagon and gear, mules, and a modest five-man military guard. He fanned out from the banks of the Smoky Hill River to ravines and creek beds where moving water had shifted bones to lower ground, scouring banks and cliffs where the elements had worn through to reveal fossils framed in stone.

Over the next few weeks, Cope feverishly collected the remains of

UNCHARTED TERRITORY

Cope found his chance to dig into the West by reaching out to the new US geological surveys the government was busy organizing after the Civil War to map uncharted frontier and take stock of natural resources.

For several years at a stretch, geologists, survey mapmakers, and other specialists, including paleontologists, trekked around the western states.

Four expeditions were in progress in the years that Cope and Marsh were most active in the West: Clarence King and his crew covered eastern Wyoming to western Nevada (1867-73), along the route of the transcontinental railroad. George Wheeler's survey (1869-79) set out to map the territory from 100 degrees west longitude to the Pacific Ocean. John Wesley Powell's survey (1870-76) explored canyons and river ways in the southwest. Powell named the Grand Canyon, and he and his team were the first explorers of European descent to raft down the Colorado River. The Hayden survey (1871-77), which would ultimately hire Cope, covered huge stretches of Nebraska, Colorado, and Wyoming, including what would become Yellowstone National Park.

plesiosaurs, mosasaurs, sea turtles, and massive fish—and yes, a fine specimen of a pterodactyl, with a wingspan of twenty-five feet.

"The stories I hear of what Marsh and others have found," he wrote Annie, "is something wonderful, and I can now tell my own stories, which for the time I have been here are not bad."

Not bad indeed, but he would need to find a way to get back—and soon.

IN SPRING 1872, HAYDEN CAME THROUGH, OFFERING COPE AN UNPAID POST AS chief paleontologist with his geological survey. The survey would meet partial expenses and give Cope leave to hunt fossils in the West, including western Wyoming and Bridger Basin. Partnering with a survey also offered the safety of numbers in a hostile political landscape, and a paid platform for publishing scientific papers about his finds.

Cope's enthusiasm took a blow when he arrived at Fort Bridger to find that Hayden's team had left without him on a trek to Yellowstone, taking all the wagons and horses with them. The fort's depleted ranks could spare no escort. Until he could scrape together enough to buy or rent his own supplies and hire men, he would be stuck bunking at night in the government hay yard. He fired off letter after imploring letter to Hayden and his father, requesting money to proceed. He waited for weeks at Fort Bridger, finally renting a house and summoning Annie and six-year-old Julia west to keep him company.

Members of Ferdinand Vandeveer Hayden's geological survey, circa 1870.

Marsh soon got wind of Cope's movements, and it rankled him. He was unusually possessive about Bridger, and soon enough Cope would find the means to get out into the field. Who knew what treasures he might scoop from under Marsh's distant gaze?

When it came to naming and describing specimens, Cope rushed—his peers agreed—and made careless mistakes. But he always showed up prepared. He read scientific papers nonstop and kept tabs on what others had found and where. He picked the brains of local amateur fossil hunters and studied their collections. Above all, he was in tune with the geologic past. He had an uncanny knack for imagining prehistoric landscapes and predicting the best dig sites.

Much as Marsh might have liked to be on hand and roll up his sleeves, he had duties at Yale, not least describing last year's bounty to keep pace with Cope's prolific pen. He took steps to hold his advantage.

Marsh hired two local men, John Chew and Sam Smith, to spend the next

GRUDGING INSPIRATION

When Cope spoke "of the wonderful animals of the earth, those of long ago and those of today," wrote one assistant, "so absorbed did he become in his subject that he talked on as if to himself, looking straight ahead and rarely turning toward me, while I listened entranced."

Cope's letters home to his father, Annie, and, increasingly, his daughter, Julia, painted a vivid picture of the ancient worlds he imagined. With a few fossil clues, he seemed able to imagine a long-vanished ecosystem simply by comparing it to the present, and his eloquence inspired artists who specialized in prehistoric themes for museums. One of the top natural history artists of the day, Charles R. Knight, collaborated with Cope at his cluttered apartment in Philadelphia. "I listened with rapt attention," he wrote later, "to the greatest conversationalist that ever graced the service of Paleontology. . . . [N]ew vistas of the life of the past opened before me. . . . I felt that I had stepped back into an ancient world."

Marsh's lifestyle encouraged a less expressive or poetic view of biological time. Throughout their parallel careers, the Yale professor was more focused and

few months collecting in Wyoming and to keep watch over—and deflect, if necessary—Cope's actions. He didn't want his competitor nosing around his prime dig sites.

patient than his younger counterpart, but Cope had more energy. He seemed to magically turn up—and start digging—wherever fossils did, zigzagging around a fast-developing nation in pursuit of trophies.

A deliberate collector, imperious and conservative, Marsh might have preferred to farm out his fieldwork or buy in fossils, freeing him to analyze bones in the comfort of his stately New Haven home, where plans for the Peabody Museum evolved daily.

The intellectually restless and high-strung Cope inspired Marsh to move swiftly and achieve more than he might have otherwise, but it would not have occurred to the busy Yale professor to be grateful.

Knight's 1897 depiction of Elasmosaurus.

Artist Charles R. Knight, 1899.

WHEN COPE AT LAST GOT HIS HANDS ON FUNDING IN JULY, HE BOUGHT HORSES and supplies and hired two assistants and a cook. The little unit made for the basin, a rough passage, but within days Cope had unearthed fossils from up to thirty species of extinct animals, many never before recorded. He sent a letter updating Annie on his good fortune but asked her not to breathe a word lest Marsh find out. His loyal wife wrote back with a development in turn: Joseph Leidy had turned up at Fort Bridger.

This should have come as no surprise: when Cope defected from the academy and went to work for Hayden's survey, it was a political strike against Leidy.

Before Cope, Hayden was sending all bone specimens to the academy in Philadelphia for analysis. Now, under the patronage of the survey, Cope worked on his own scientific behalf, which meant no more fossils for Leidy. His supply was diverted, just as Cope's had been when Marsh re-routed fossils from the Haddonfield marl fields to Yale.

Cope must have felt a certain poetic justice in asserting his independence from Leidy, who had both created and—without meaning to—nearly trampled Cope's young reputation, the latter by siding with Marsh when Cope put his *Elasmosaurus*'s head on wrong. Though Leidy had really been siding with science, the perceived slight bruised Cope's loyalty.

When Leidy objected to the new arrangement, Hayden wrote back:

> I asked [Cope] not to go into that field that you were going there. He laughed at the idea of being restricted to any locality and said he intended to go whether I aided him or not, I was anxious to secure the cooperation of such a worker as an honor to my corps. I could not be responsible for the field he selected in as much as I pay him no salary and a portion of his expenses. You will see therefore that while it is not a pleasant thing to work in competition with others it seems almost a necessity. You can sympathize.

Not wishing to bump into Leidy or reveal anything, Cope migrated to a site several miles away.

Here, in July, he made a startling discovery in a nest of fossil leaves: the monstrous bones of a dinosaur he would name *Agathaumas sylvestris* ("marvelous forest dweller"). There were enough fragments to deduce that, at six tons, this was the biggest dinosaur yet discovered in North America.

Drunk on success, Cope kept up a relentless pace, rising before the sun and hunting fossils until inky darkness settled over the basin. He spent evenings in his tent examining bones by lantern light and writing—always writing—making the occasional brief foray into Fort Bridger for supplies or to mail scientific papers and visit with Annie and Julia.

When Cope's assistants proved all but useless, he fired them, adding a wayward and chatty local named Sam Smith to his payroll instead. The mutinous Smith had worked for Marsh, of course, but claimed to be unhappy in the other camp. Cope had no reason to doubt his word: Marsh had a reputation for not paying his workers on time—or, in some cases, at all. Smith might also prove a useful resource, with inside information.

Back at Yale, Marsh stewed as word arrived from Bridger. He fired off an angry telegram to which Smith, in his defense, claimed he'd only tried to distract the enemy from "good bone contry close hear" and to spy on the competition. Cope "took his meals at Manleys, hi toned for a bone sharp," Smith reported, hinting that dining out was an indulgence for the average bone hunter.

But for Marsh, Smith's motives were beside the point. Busybody Cope had sidelined Leidy—now *also* digging at Bridger!—had hired Marsh's man out from under him, and was naming species like mad.

Though Marsh had been planning to leave oversight of southwestern Wyoming to his hired men and lead a small expedition into western Kansas, he couldn't bear to have Smith and Cope in cahoots or to be outside the fray.

He penciled Fort Bridger back into his itinerary.

Yale College Scientific Expedition 1872

8

Hydra-Headed

"*I was never so angry in my life.*" —O. C. MARSH

Though he left home reluctantly, Marsh the outdoorsman enjoyed the rigors of frontier life and bristled at any suggestion that he might be a pampered eastern professor.

He got his chance to gloat not long after he stepped off the train at Fort Wallace in his old slouch hat and corduroy suit, his pockets drooping with fossils. Marsh and his band of four Yale students, a Mexican guide, and an army lieutenant and escort had just made camp when someone in the party spotted a distant herd of buffalo, some one hundred thousand animals, more than any of the men had ever seen in one place. "The broad valley before us, perhaps, six or eight miles wide," wrote Marsh, "was black with buffalo."

When he rode down on his trusty pony, Pawnee, to hunt up supper for the camp, sporting a "cavalry carbine and a pair of navy revolvers" and targeting

The third Yale expedition led by O. C. Marsh, 1872.

his prey "in the exact manner my first guide, Buffalo Bill, had taught me," the sudden gunfire set the herd in motion. Before Marsh knew it, they were all hurtling toward him.

He steered Pawnee along with the thundering buffalo, and the brave pony galloped and weaved and minced to avoid prairie dog holes that might have snared a hoof and spelled their doom.

Still galloping miles later to keep from being trampled in the stampede, Marsh spotted a butte ahead and maneuvered Pawnee behind it while thundering buffalo streamed around the bloodied and exhausted horse and rider.

Marsh even managed to shoot a buffalo for supper.

THE CAVALIER PROFESSOR'S LUCK HELD DURING A brief field stop in the Smoky Hill River region of western Kansas.

That dig yielded several large, flightless birds, one nearly intact. It was all there, apart from the skull, and would have stood nearly six feet tall. But what made *Hesperornis regalis* ("royal western bird")—as Marsh would name his find—rare and exciting was its mouthful of teeth. No bird alive has teeth, so an extinct bird with reptilian traits was big news in the scientific community, further narrowing the gap between birds and reptiles and lending vital support to Darwin's theory of evolution.

Leaving Fort Wallace again, the Marsh team made a stop at Fort D. A. Russell, at last reaching Bridger Basin in mid-August.

Cope, who would have known Marsh was coming, had moved camp with a reduced entourage of three men and four pack mules.

The position of the two digs, just miles apart, allowed their zealous leaders to both avoid and monitor one another. Cope even looked in on one combed-over Marsh site, finding abandoned fragments of skull and loose teeth. Had his nemesis overlooked the specimen? Earnest as always, Cope scooped it up.

He would go ahead and describe the fossil, only to learn two decades later that the remains had belonged to two separate (and already described) species. Someone on the Marsh team had toyed with him, planting the prize to lead Cope astray.

Peabody Museum cast of the famous "Berlin Specimen," Archaeopteryx lithographica.

THE FIRST BIRD

A little over a year after Darwin published *On the Origin of Species*, one of the most important fossils ever found was unearthed in the Jurassic Solnhofen Limestone of southern Germany.

Unlike living birds, *Archaeopteryx lithographica* ("Ancient wing") had a full set of teeth, a flat breastbone, and a long, bony tail. It also had feathers, feathered wings, and other characteristics of birds today, making it an extinct "transitional" form between bird and reptile, an "intermediate" between the winged creatures we see daily and predatory dinosaurs like *Deinonychus*.

It was also hard evidence of evolution in action, though not all scientists accepted its implications.

Important new evidence came in the form of Marsh's 1871 discovery of *Hesperornis regalis* and publication of *Odontornithes: A Monograph on the Extinct Toothed Birds of North America* (a study of the Cretaceous birds of Kansas), which brought him more fame and acclaim than any other discovery or pursuit.

FOR THE REST OF AUGUST, COPE AND MARSH TOILED A FEW MILES APART without meeting. Leidy avoided them both. All three were aware of the comings and goings of the others and that they were digging in deposits of about the same age. There was bound to be overlap. Yet the wary trio didn't collaborate, didn't communicate, and didn't hesitate to duplicate their efforts.

By September, Leidy and Marsh had returned east, while Cope kept up his usual relentless pace, literally making himself sick in the bargain. He told his family he would soon "close up the expedition and sell out. . . . The season here is autumnal; sometimes ice and snow are not far off."

But it wasn't until supplies were scant and Cope—who liked to spread his blanket under a stand of willows and fall asleep "looking up at Cassiopeia and listening to the yelping of coyotes"—started waking to blankets crisp with frost and ice in the company's canteens that he broke down camp.

He staggered back to Fort Bridger around the middle of September with a ragged chest cough. A dangerous fever soon followed, one that didn't let up for weeks, leaving Annie to nurse her husband, care for their young daughter, Julia, pen and post Cope's letters and descriptions, chase Hayden for expedition financing, and appease the landlady—a woman handy with curse words that made a modest Quaker bride blush.

Annie nursed a "very weak & helpless" Cope through delirium and nightmares until he was well enough (if exhausted and broke) to travel home at the end of October.

BY LATE FALL OF 1872, ALL THREE PALEONTOLOGISTS WERE PUBLISHING ARTICLES about their discoveries at Bridger Basin.

With each man racing to name and class his fossils before his opponents, many species ended up with three different scientific names, a tangle it would take the scientific community years to unravel.

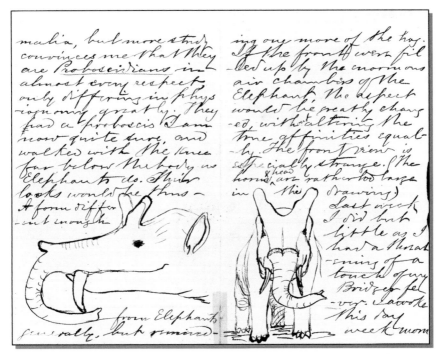

Cope, Marsh, and Leidy all unearthed skulls of the same animal in Wyoming's Bridger Basin but gave it different scientific names. In this letter to his father, Cope sketched the creature as he imagined it at the time, with a trunk.

The Bridger blitz—so many competing discoveries in an age without publication standards, or a panel to arbitrate disputes—had unleashed scientific chaos. Marsh and Cope squabbled bitterly over priority while Leidy tried to sort through and dodge the crossfire.

When Cope sent Marsh a polite letter along with some of Marsh's specimens that had accidentally routed to him at the academy, he took the opportunity to congratulate his colleague—"your bird with teeth is simply delightful"—to which Marsh replied, "I am glad you fully appreciated my bird with teeth and I hope soon to send you some photographs of it."

But from there he launched an offensive: "I was so mad at you for getting away Smith (to whom I had given valuable notes about localities etc.) I should have 'gone for you' not with pistols or fists, but in print. . . . I was never

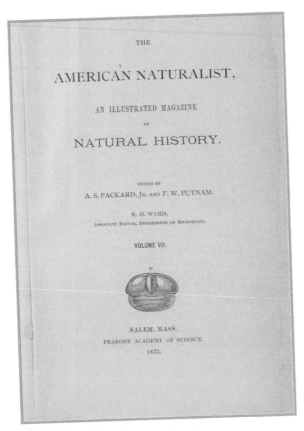

The American Naturalist magazine title page, 1873.

so angry in my life." He asked Cope to reply with equal frankness, and it took Cope four pages to do so, at the end of which he requested that Marsh retract his accusations of impropriety.

Marsh wouldn't budge, though he wanted to remain friends if possible. "I feel I have been deeply wronged by you in numerous instances. . . . After the Smith affair last summer, I made up my mind that forbearance was no longer a virtue."

Around the same time, a colleague wrote to Leidy: "[Marsh] seems hot on the path of Professor Cope, and says he will expose his . . . villanies!! Won't he have a pretty large job for one person?"

At first, the struggle was confined to belligerent letters back and forth, each man accusing the other of manufacturing data or fudging dates, but soon the sniping started to appear in scientific journals. By January 1873 a war of words had broken out, most notably in the esteemed *The American Naturalist*.

In the journal's March 1873 issue, Cope proposed that uintatheres, a fossil all three scientists had found variations on, was an ancestor of modern elephants.

"Prof. Cope . . . has made several serious mistakes in his observations," a haughty Marsh shot back in print, compiling them in exhaustive detail.

Marsh petitioned to get Cope's erroneous papers withdrawn from the record, and—always one up on the brash Philadelphian politically—seemed close to succeeding.

Weighing his attacker's chances of success in a letter to his father, Cope complained, "Marsh has always been extraordinarily jealous, and it would seem to have at last developed into insanity."

By spring of 1873, editors at the *The American Naturalist* had had it. In the June issue, they invited both paleontologists to publish a concluding statement at their own expense: "We regret that Professors Marsh and Cope have considered it necessary to carry their controversy to the extent that they have. . . . [It] has come to be a personal one. . . . [T]he *Naturalist* is not called upon to devote further space to its consideration."

Cope sent one brisk paragraph; Marsh, nine pages—his most vicious attack yet. "Prof. Cope's errors will continue to invite correction," he proposed, "but these, like his blunders, are hydra-headed, and life is really too short to spend valuable time in such an ungracious task."

Leidy, meanwhile, in his quiet, unassuming way, was busy comparing the most disputed fossils. It soon became clear that his *Uintatherium*, Marsh's *Tinoceras* and *Dinoceras*, and Cope's *Loxolophodon* were different names for the same creature.

After publishing his analysis, Leidy lost heart and began to distance himself from his rivals and from paleontology in general. Civil and rational, he couldn't accept or condone slapdash science and lacked the resources, temperament, and greed to keep pace. "Formerly, every fossil one found in the States came to me," Leidy told a British colleague, "for nobody else cared to study such things, but Professors Marsh and Cope, with long purses, offer money for what used to come to me for nothing. . . . I cannot compete."

Too careful and considerate for a field where everything was outsize—big fossils, big stakes, big egos—Leidy would live out his remaining career on the far side of the scientific spectrum, studying single-celled microorganisms.

Leidy's gradual retreat gave Cope and Marsh more leave to sharpen their claws. As their bitter and increasingly public conflict wore on, other scientists, agog with disbelief, began to wince and withdraw from the spectacle. No one had witnessed anything quite like it before.

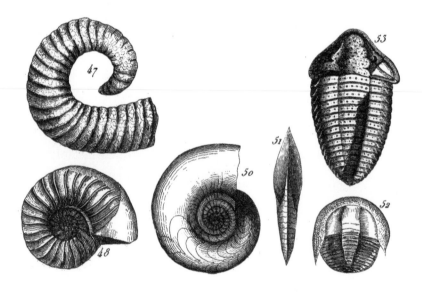

A BRASH YOUNG SCIENCE

Writer and humorist Mark Twain nicknamed the last three decades (or so) of the nineteenth century "the Gilded Age." America after the Civil War was a brash young country in recovery and in thrall to money.

The rapid growth of industry—railroads, factories, mining, finance—combined with huge waves of immigration and urbanization, as people flooded into US cities chasing opportunity and better wages, triggered an economic boom. Fortunes surged and speculation was rampant. Everyone wanted a slice of the pie, but not everyone got one. People with money—captains of industry or financiers like John D. Rockefeller of Standard Oil, Andrew Carnegie of Carnegie Steel, and banker J. P. Morgan—had loads of it, together with enormous power and influence. Those who had little had very little, resulting in grave social ills and inequity.

Paleontology as Cope and Marsh knew it, as a quest for bigger and better dinosaurs, reflected the times they lived in, when ambition and ruthless competition went hand in hand.

Even after the "bone wars" of Cope and Marsh began to fade from public memory, wealthy patrons like Andrew Carnegie stoked the fire of competition between curators and field collectors.

When dinosaur fever hit another milestone near the end of the century, the celebrity philanthropist knew he had to have one of these towering beasts for his museum in Pittsburgh; he also knew how to promote his prize once he got it: *Diplodocus carnegii* and other big-ticket specimens at Carnegie's museum of natural history—*Apatosaurus*, *Triceratops*, *Stegosaurus*, *Allosaurus*—would become world famous.

Andrew Carnegie, 1913.

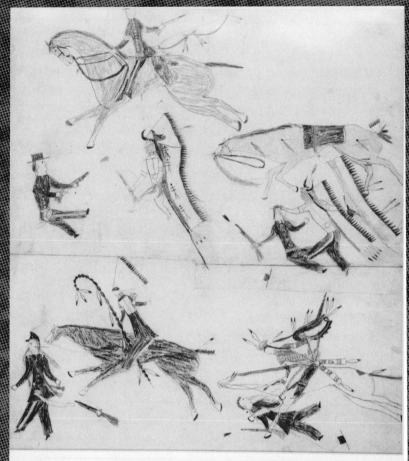

Gefechtsszene zwischen Sioux-Indianern und Unionstruppen. Der Autor der Zeichnung, der Sioux Shunka-
wapa „Das schwarze Roß" fegtinen fort einem einem Soldaten den Scalp genommen.

CHAPTER

9

Wariness and Controversy

*"I wish they would stop their race and work quietly.
I have told Marsh more than once that it would
do more for his reputation among zoologists to
describe one species thoroughly than be the one to
name a hundred."* —GEOLOGIST JAMES DWIGHT DANA

Like Marsh, Cope admitted their feud was a waste of valuable professional energy. "My time is too fully occupied in more important subjects," he countered, "to permit me to waste it upon personal affairs which are sufficiently before the public."

Things did in fact simmer down with the summer collecting season at hand.

Marsh organized a third Yale-sponsored dig with eleven students and two scouts, focused on Nebraska's Niobrara River.

With Sioux–US Army tensions running high, Cope postponed a trip to the Dakota Badlands and set his sights on Colorado.

Battle between Sioux and Union troops: drawing by Sitting Bull, before 1890.

Busy though he was, Marsh couldn't get Cope off the brain. He hired Ervin Devendorf to explore an area near Cope's Colorado camp, bullying his man constantly for updates. "I have been making inquiries," Devendorf reported, reassuring Marsh that there were more rumors than successes.

Marsh's team unearthed more prehistoric horses and other notable mammal fossils before revisiting Bridger Basin, returning to New Haven that fall with forty-nine crates of fossils. Marsh appealed to Hayden not to publish Cope's expedition papers, writing a seven-page complaint to the survey sponsor demanding "simple justice." Hayden, who had once (in a letter to Leidy) referred to Cope as a "mule head," proved a loyal proponent of his employee's work all the same. He politely declined, and Marsh had a new enemy.

In the spring of 1874, Marsh's political savvy got him elected to membership in the prestigious National Academy of Sciences (NAS). (Cope's was the only "no" vote.) He began networking in earnest with key scientists and policy makers, staying behind in New Haven that summer to publish, prepare specimens, and supervise construction of the Peabody Museum.

COPE, MEANWHILE, JOINED FORCES WITH THE WHEELER SURVEY OF THE SOUTH-west led by George Montague Wheeler. The pay was better than Hayden could offer, and it gave Cope freedom to explore unknown terrain near the San Juan River in New Mexico. In one five-day dig alone, he unearthed fossil remains of seventy-five species.

Marsh had a pleasant surprise of his own in October: an army general alerted him to extensive deposits near White River in northern Nebraska and southern Dakota territory. From Fort McPherson, Nebraska, Marsh and his team traveled in search of horses and wagons to the Red Cloud Agency, a government office near the reservation where Chief Red Cloud and a large band of Oglala Lakota had settled.

Red Cloud's warriors had soundly defeated US Army troops in Wyoming and agreed afterward to a settlement treaty. To maintain peace and gain land concessions for the army, the agency now provided food and supplies for the tribe. It was a flawed arrangement from the start, and by the time Marsh and his team arrived, agency officials were steeped in corruption, rations were grim, and the Oglala were living in deprivation. Assuming Marsh and his men wanted to prospect for gold, the Sioux furiously demanded their departure.

Chief Red Cloud, circa 1880.

The relationship between Native leaders and white scientists had changed dramatically since the 1850s and 1860s. When Plains Indians in Wyoming, Montana, and the Dakotas first spotted Ferdinand Vandeveer Hayden collecting in the field (often, in those days, for Leidy and the academy), they had pegged Cope's future survey boss as a harmless white lunatic. They called the man who carried no weapon and pawed restlessly at the ground "He Who Picks Up Stones Running" and paid him no mind. But by the time Marsh arrived at the Red Cloud Agency, paleontologists and other white scientist-explorers—and their motives—were deeply suspect.

Ever the politician, Marsh threw a banquet for Red Cloud and other tribal leaders, and stated his case. It was bones he was after, not gold. He would pay Indian scouts to assist the expedition and use his connections in Washington to advocate for the tribe.

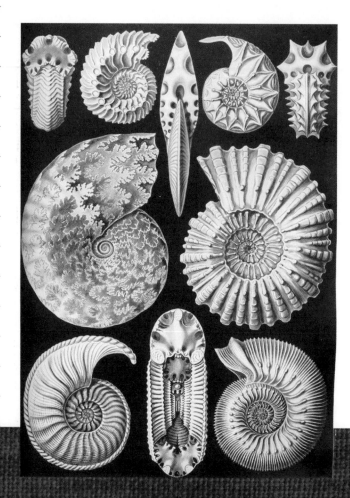

At first, the Sioux agreed, though wariness and controversy prevailed. In the end, impatient Marsh just set off in the dead of night, directing his party stealthily past Indian lodges while the inhabitants slept.

It was a tense, cold trek, but he and his escort managed to lead the team into the White River Badlands (today a portion of Badlands National Park in South Dakota) with its eroded limestone bluffs and ravines.

Scientists often use fossil ammonite shells, which are abundant and present in different geological epochs, to date other fossils.

ALL KINDS OF BEINGS WERE CHANGED TO STONE

Long before the colonists, before Columbus, Native Americans formed their own ideas about the mysterious remains of extinct creatures. Native tribes wove fossils into myths and creation stories, using the stony teeth and claws in ceremonial magic and protections and for trade. In Sioux mythology, *Pteranodon*-like Thunder Birds battle long-necked Water Monsters. Plains Indians used iridescent marine fossils (long ago, shallow ocean waters covered much of inland North America, including the Great Plains) to magically summon buffalo herds.

"All kinds of beings were changed to stone," Zuni elders observed in 1891. "We find . . . their forms, sometimes large like the beings themselves, sometimes shriveled and distorted. We often see

The site lay in a deep gorge, and it was true! There were bones for miles. His team worked at a furious pace to stay warm, dusting during snow squalls to keep the fossils visible. Marsh snapped icicles from his beard at mealtime and obsessed over Cope's progress in Colorado. He bullied his man Devendorf for updates. The spy had found a site earmarked by Cope for the next season. "Those marks are now defaced by the sole of my boot," he assured his boss, "but I know where they were."

Marsh's team would leave the Badlands with some two tons of fossils, many "rare specimens, illustrative of entire classes of quadrupeds."

All the while, Indian sentries rode in and out of camp by day, keeping an eye on things, or lingered beyond the camp circle at night.

Danger and discomfort did little to distract Marsh from thinking about what mischief Cope might be up to and didn't keep him from gloating. An infantry major saw him pause at one point to consider a bone jutting out of a bank they rode past on a side outing: Marsh turned his horse, leaped down, and made a beeline for the fossil. He "dug around the specimen awhile, then among the rocks the forms of many beings that live no longer."

Native perspectives on fossils were as various as tribal bloodlines, passed down orally through generations, over centuries; but almost all were at home with the idea of what geologists call "deep time," a consciousness of the earth's age.

When formal science first took an interest in discoveries like the Ice Age fossils of Kentucky's Big Bone Lick (studied by Benjamin Franklin, Daniel Boone, and Cuvier in France, among others), bone hunters took the time to record Native traditions, which informed major concepts in geology and paleontology and helped shape Cuvier's theory of catastrophic extinctions.

But by the time Marsh and Cope brought their rivalry west, such documentation and collaboration had tapered off, though white collectors often hired Native guides to lead them to bone beds or shelter them from hostile tribes.

As bone hunters fanned out later in the century, seizing fossils for eastern museums, the plunder of fossils, artifacts, and human remains by the government and museums set off a controversy that continues to this day, a dramatic example being the federal seizure of a priceless *Tyrannosaurus* skeleton named Sue recovered on contested land in 1990 (and the legal "custody" battle that followed).

suddenly seemed to have gone crazy. He danced, swung his hat in the air, and yelled, 'I've got him, I've got him.'" The professor was "having an exciting controversy with a rival scientist," the major understood, "about a prehistoric animal which both claimed to have discovered and named." Marsh had scored.

On their last day in the White River Badlands, a party of Red Cloud's men galloped into camp with an alert: a war party from the north was on the move, and would likely attack that night.

Marsh could either stay and pack up—and risk life and limb, and the lives of his men—or flee to safe haven and ditch his discoveries. He chose to stay.

His team worked feverishly through the night to secure the fossils and ready the wagons for travel, and the convoy hastened back to the Red Cloud Agency.

The war party had, they were told, missed the expedition by hours.

And so ended another collecting season in the West.

Cope spent the summer of 1875 home in Haddonfield, preparing the San Juan River fossils. He didn't welcome the respite but knew he had to sort,

BIG BONE CHIEF

When Marsh turned up in 1874 to dig in the rich fossil beds east of the Black Hills, in what is today Badlands National Park, he needed permission from the Lakota. He never got it. Tribal leaders were outraged at the time by a broken treaty—and subsequent government incursion into sacred territory—and though some supported his request, they couldn't reach consensus.

Marsh slipped past and dug anyway, escaping with his life (and his fossils) only with the assistance of his ally Chief Red Cloud.

Marsh did honor his pledge to put tribal grievances before President Grant. In lobbying on behalf of the Lakota in Washington, Marsh triggered a scandal over government corruption—and Native American rights—that reached into the White House and would later lead to reforms.

Red Cloud would always remember this gesture, just as Marsh would Red

name, and announce his discoveries or else fall behind in the great race to name new species.

When his father died that year, Cope lost his closest intellectual confidant, but together with sorrow came liberation. Alfred had long controlled the family purse strings and looked on his son's scientific pursuits with caution. He left Edward a fortune.

Cope could now direct the course of his own life and fund his work. He bought two houses next door to one another in Philadelphia. He, Annie, and Julia would have one; the fossils, the other.

He also followed Marsh's lead and hired professional help to keep pace with his rival's men in the Kansas plains.

Charles Sternberg would prove to be one of Cope's most loyal and industrious assistants. "I put my soul in the letter I wrote him," Sternberg later remembered, "for this was my last chance. . . . I told him of my love for science, and my earnest longing to enter the chalk of western Kansas . . . no matter what it might cost me in discomfort and danger . . . I was too poor to go at my own expense."

Cloud's warning. When the chief came east on a diplomatic mission in 1883, he paid a call in New Haven.

Red Cloud spoke of Marsh as the "Big Bone Chief" and praised his honor: "He told the Great Father everything just as he promised he would, and I think he is the best white man I ever saw."

O. C. Marsh with Chief Red Cloud in New Haven, Connecticut, circa 1883.

Deciding to take a chance on this earnest if inexperienced bone hound, Cope sent young Sternberg a $300 bank draft. "I like your style," his note read. "Go to work."

Sternberg did, toiling in seclusion with little rest. He was acutely aware of Marsh's hired men, Benjamin Mudge and Samuel Williston, who were digging just a few miles away, and spied on them when he could, informing Cope of their doings and discoveries.

Charles Sternberg in the field, circa 1926.

Mudge and Williston, in turn, kept a watch on Sternberg. The lone bone hunter was often so worried about leaving his site exposed, even for a few hours, that he went without food. At one point, with eight hundred pounds of mosasaur to pry from the rock-hard earth, and enemies everywhere, Sternberg ate nothing but boiled corn for three days running.

At the end of July, Cope hired J. C. Isaac from Wyoming and summoned both young assistants to Omaha. He would abandon Kansas for now and light out for Montana's Judith River Basin.

This was a bold—some might say foolhardy—proposition in 1876.

In June, Lakota, Northern Cheyenne, and Arapaho forces led by Sitting Bull and Crazy Horse had combined to annihilate the cavalry forces led by George Custer at Little Bighorn. Sternberg himself had seen wide columns of Cheyenne migrating through Kansas to join Sitting Bull.

"The professor was strongly advised against the folly of going into the neutral ground between the Sioux and their hereditary enemies, the Crows," Sternberg wrote. "A member of either tribe might kill us, and lay our death on the other tribe."

But even six weeks after Custer's Last Stand, Cope pressed on. He was convinced that the Sioux would be in council with Sitting Bull until forced north by gathering US troops. His team would be safe at least through

THE BATTLE OF THE LITTLE BIGHORN

The Black Hills of South Dakota are Lakota sacred ground, and in the summer of 1874, the US Army violated an 1868 treaty made with Oglala Lakota Chief Red Cloud and dispatched cavalry into the hills to investigate rumors of gold.

The invasion outraged Chiefs Sitting Bull and Crazy Horse, who had long opposed government attempts to force their people onto reservations, and the betrayal prompted other tribes to join Sitting Bull in Montana.

By the late spring of 1876, more than ten thousand defiant Native Americans had pitched camp along the Little Bighorn River in a show of solidarity, despite a US War Department order demanding retreat. In a sun dance ritual, Sitting Bull experienced a vision of soldiers falling into the Lakota camp like grasshoppers from the sky, inspiring Crazy Horse and his warriors to attack advancing US troops, forcing their retreat.

The bloody conflict, which the Plains Indians call the Battle of the Greasy Grass (and others call Custer's Last Stand), took place in June 1876, when the Seventh Cavalry Regiment of the US Army, including a force led by Lieutenant

Colonel George Armstrong Custer, counterattacked the encampment near southern Montana's Little Bighorn River.

The combined forces of the Lakota, Northern Cheyenne, and Arapaho under Crazy Horse and Sitting Bull won a decisive victory in a fierce battle that wiped out five of the Seventh Cavalry's twelve companies and killed Custer.

General George Custer, 1865. Chief Sitting Bull, 1883.

An 1889 stagecoach.

summer, and free to collect to their hearts' content. He had a strong intuition about the Judith River Basin.

But first they had to get there. When he stepped off the train on August 1, 1876, leaning heavily on Annie, Cope's new hires must have wondered what they were in for. Their mentor, who suffered frequent "attacks of fever" throughout his exploring career, "was so weak," Sternberg wrote, "that he reeled from side to side when he walked."

Could this frail man survive Montana wilderness (there wasn't even a rail line yet!), much less lead an ambitious expedition into dangerous territory?

But the "mule head" in Cope served him well on the frontier, and after leaving Annie off in Ogden, Utah, to catch her train back to Philadelphia, the party continued on by rail to Franklin, Idaho, to connect with the next leg of the journey—a dreaded stagecoach.

The trio camped on the train platform and boarded the morning stage to Helena, a four-day trip.

Stagecoach travel was a jarring, rattling, crowded, dusty, sleepless ordeal. For fear of bandits, Cope had sewn his money into his pant legs. Near the end of the jaunt, they found themselves at the mercy of a wildly drunk replacement driver named (surprise) Whiskey Jack.

When they arrived in the bustling frontier capital of Montana, everyone was abuzz about Custer. But stubborn Cope, very much on the mend here under Big Sky, pushed on. Isaac, who had lost five companions in Wyoming earlier that year to Indian attacks, had serious qualms, but both assistants stood bravely by their leader.

The team arrived at remote Fort Benton, which Sternberg described as a "typical frontier town . . . streets paved with playing cards and whiskey for sale."

Cope was warned yet again not to blunder out into the Missouri River Valley: there were a couple thousand Sioux fighters out there and more than three thousand soldiers in hot pursuit.

Before leaving the safety of the fort, Cope wrote to reassure Annie: "Everyone considers [the rumors of Sioux coming through] false. . . . Everybody including Captain Williams who is commandant at the fort says there is no danger in the region to which I am going."

It took another week, but at last the team—now with a guide and cook, "the best I ever had," Cope gushed to Annie—found themselves comfortably situated in the badlands along the Missouri River. There was "splendid grass as far as the eye could reach" and a landscape plentiful in "buffalo, antelope, deer, wolves, Indians etc." Cope thought this the best camp and crew he could recall, though the last item on that list may have given Annie pause under the political circumstances, along with Cope's reference to a nearby camp of "some 30 lodges of some Indians I do not know."

But Cope paid these neighbors a visit the following day and found a large tribe of peaceful Crow. He invited several elders to dinner, and "they were greatly amused," he reported, "to see me take out my teeth & put them back in." This congenial tribe—all one thousand or so—moved on a day after the encounter, most likely to follow the buffalo, but their sudden absence must have caused Cope's team unease.

The fossils they were finding in the Judith River Basin were an odd mix of mainly reptiles and fish, with the occasional *really* big bone thrown in. These fossils were often isolated and too fragile to unearth, so broken as to be "not worth digging out." But their presence posed a mystery.

Answers were around the bend (as one peer put it, Cope's 1876 trip would show "that dinosaurs had been present in the West in considerable abundance in Cretaceous times, although his material gave little hint of their skeletal structure or of their immense size"), but for now Cope was even more perplexed by some of what they were unearthing than he had been by the bounty in the San Juan Basin.

The idyllic camp conditions he'd described to Annie fast gave way to hardship.

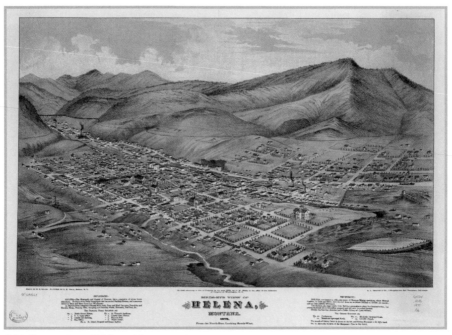

A bird's-eye view of Helena, Montana, 1875.

The rented horses proved half-wild. The badlands water was alkaline and thick with mud. The heat could surge out of nowhere, and the food, however tasty, didn't agree with Cope. The roving of his restless mind—or perhaps indigestion—inflicted noisy nightmares, which Sternberg woke him from. Relentless swarms of gnats got under their horses' saddles and the men's hats and sleeves, leaving scabby sores and forcing them to slather their faces in bacon grease to repel the attacks.

But Cope was also the first to rise and the last to go to sleep—always curious, always seeking. "I have never known a more wonderful example," his faithful assistant Sternberg wrote, "of the will's power over the body."

The Judith River bluffs were higher than those in the White River, the canyons steep and disorienting, full of cliffs and dark chasms, and it was easy to lose your footing or get turned around, which Isaac did one day: "The lands are very confused," Cope wrote, "a labyrinth of gorges & precipices & I found that he had fallen down and injured himself."

They found in the high rocks bones and teeth of familiar animals like *Laelaps* and *Hadrosaurus*, but also fragments of an unknown rhino-like beast, and Cope was seeing an ecosystem in his mind's eye. As in the San Juan River Valley, Cope's uncanny knack for imagining prehistoric landscapes and predicting a prime site would serve him well in the Judith River Basin. His crew unearthed some twenty-one new species, mainly from fossil teeth, not to mention the world's first tremendous horned dinosaur: *Monoclonius* ("single sprout") *crassus* ("the fat one").

But the seeking came at great risk. Those half-wild horses saved the men's lives by sensing, one dark night, the edge of a ten-foot-wide gorge that would have sent them hurtling one hundred feet to their deaths.

CHAPTER

Another Name for Truth

> *"No collection . . . approaches that made by*
> *Professor Marsh, in completeness of the chain of*
> *evidence."*
> —THOMAS HUXLEY

"We are up to our knees in Eocene mud," Marsh boasted as he and his colleagues at the new Peabody Museum of Natural History unpacked crate after crate from Kansas.

For some time, Marsh had taken a focused and purposeful approach to collecting. Birds with teeth and prehistoric horses held more value, he believed, than the remains of random monsters, and occupied him more than fieldwork. To keep pace with the competition, he relied on teams to do his collecting. Paleontology was an increasingly ruthless field, and Marsh suffered no fools. Key loyalists like Benjamin Mudge pledged discretion and utter secrecy, going to great lengths to please their exacting master.

Along with the seemingly endless stream of mastodons and pterodactyls,

Editorial cartoon of Charles Darwin depicted as an ape, 1871.

Mudge sent word that Marsh's nemesis was even now digging in Sioux country, where US troops were in hot pursuit of Sitting Bull's men. How reckless, the Yale professor must have thought. How mule-headed.

Safe in his museum in New Haven, Marsh was expecting an important visitor.

English biologist Thomas Huxley, an expert on the genealogy of horses, known as "Darwin's Bulldog" because of his eloquent and aggressive defense of the other scientist and his theories, was possibly the most famous scientist of the day.

He had sailed to New York that August for a highly anticipated lecture series on evolution at Manhattan's Chickering Hall the following month. Huxley's visit would be front-page news, along with continuing coverage of Custer's demise and the fate of the Sioux.

But first, the great scientist would stop in Philadelphia to see Leidy and *Hadrosaurus* and at Yale to see Marsh's work.

Over the course of his career, Marsh had built and nurtured one fossil group in particular. What Huxley didn't yet know was that Marsh's collection

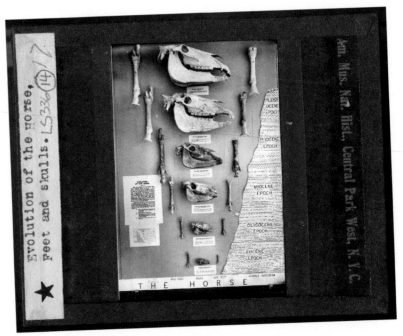

Fossils illustrating the evolution of the horse. Darwin's branching model and modern evolutionary theory no longer support such a linear view, but Marsh's equine collection certainly impressed Huxley.

of horse skeletons, nicely rounded out by his recent Antelope Junction finds, now formed an almost continuous fossil record dating back to the Eocene.

He had stitched together a sixty-million-year-old story of the horse and its evolution from a fox-sized ancestor to the horse of today, showing how several toes had morphed into only one (a single hoof) and how the animal's teeth had gradually evolved to suit a grassland environment.

The bones were so well documented, they could work as index fossils: paleontologists could determine how old a layer of earth was just by identifying the horse remains unearthed in that layer.

The collection was more than a snapshot of anatomical evolution; it showed the transformation of the earth itself. The West in Eocene times was dense forest, perfect for the little, foxy horse; by the Pleistocene, it was wind-swept prairie, an ideal home for *Equus*, equipped with thundering hooves and large, flat teeth for grazing.

"My excellent host met me at the station," Huxley wrote his wife, "and it seems he could not make enough of me. . . . I am installed in apartments which were occupied by his uncle, the millionaire Peabody, and am as quiet as if I were in my own house."

From nine to six every day during Huxley's visit, Marsh regaled him with pterodactyls, mosasaurs, plesiosaurs, and many other ancient species, but there was one collection Huxley wanted to see above all.

Darwin and his followers acknowledged the gaps in the fossil record. There seemed no realistic way to fill them; there were too many missing links between stages. But Marsh's collection appeared to have no gaps. Here for the first time, Huxley believed, was hard, physical proof of evolution. As they took their lunch or evening tea or rode in a carriage down the elm-lined avenues of New Haven, Huxley concluded, as he would tell his wife in a letter, "[Marsh] is a wonderfully good fellow, full of fun and stories about his western adventures, and the collection of fossils is the most wonderful thing I ever saw."

The English scientist had used the horse as an example of evolution as early as 1870, and Marsh knew Huxley planned to address the animal's genealogy in his lecture. "My own explorations had led me to conclusions quite

DARWIN'S BULLDOG

"Is man an ape or an angel?" demanded one critic, after reading Charles Darwin's "dangerous" book. "My Lord, I am on the side of the angels. I repudiate with indignation and abhorrence these new-fangled theories."

Scientists were as divided on the subject of evolution by natural selection as everyone else. One of the most outspoken critics was Richard Owen, the very anatomist who'd coined the term "dinosaur." Head of the natural history collections at the British Museum at the time, Owen loudly rejected aspects of the theory, demanding more substantial evidence.

An influential biologist in his own right, Thomas Huxley couldn't be more unlike his friend Darwin. He loved a good debate and pledged his support in an 1859 letter:

> I finished your book yesterday. . . .
> No work on Natural History . . .
> has made so great an impression
> upon me. . . . As for your doctrines
> I am prepared to go to the Stake if
> requisite. . . . I am sharpening up
> my claws & beak in readiness.

A popular speaker who could break complex subjects down for the general public, Huxley happily sparred with Owen and other critics, lectured widely on the theory, and went to bat for Darwin in the press. (The public eagerly followed the debate over "the monkey theory." When Darwin saw a pamphlet of Huxley's lectures, he lamented, "What is the good of my writing a thundering big book, when everything is in this green little book, so despicable for its size?")

Marsh would take great pride in his association with Huxley, calling him a "guide, philosopher, and friend, almost from the time I made the choice of science as my life work."

BONES AND STONES, AND SUCH LIKE THINGS.

different from his," he explained later, "and my specimens seemed to prove to me conclusively that the horse originated in the New World, not the Old."

When he proposed the idea, Huxley resisted, but in response to every argument the visitor made, Marsh sent an assistant to fetch a box to prove his point. "I believe you are a magician," Huxley teased. "Whatever I want, you just conjure up."

Two days later, Huxley confessed: he was now fully convinced that horses had evolved not in the Old World but in the New. Marsh's data showed the evolution of the horse without a doubt, spelling out the direct line of descent of a living creature for the first time.

During his historic address, Huxley predicted that one day, remains of a little horse with five toes, one that might even have galloped among the dinosaurs, would be dug up from an even earlier Eocene deposit. In Marsh's office, the two men had joked about this, and Huxley sketched a cartoon of his take on that first horse, which he named *Eohippus*. Marsh asked him to draw a rider, and Huxley added *Eohomo*, a very hairy rider.

"Seldom has prophecy been sooner fulfilled," Huxley would later write his son. Within seven weeks of Huxley's visit, "Professor Marsh had described a new genus of equine mammals, *Eohippus* ['dawn horse'], from the lowest Eocene deposits of the West."

The specimen had been right there all along, waiting in an unopened crate in the Peabody Museum.

Home in England, Huxley wrote to thank Marsh, and added, "I am thinking of discoursing on the birds with teeth. Have you anything new to tell on that subject? I have implicit faith in the inexhaustibility of the contents of those boxes."

A caricature of biologist Thomas Huxley, 1872.

Thomas Huxley's sketch of five-toed Eohippus *(ridden by "Eohomo"), presented to his host after viewing Marsh's groundbreaking collection of fossil horses, 1876.*

Birds with teeth! If Marsh could replicate his success with horses in *that* collection, he'd demonstrate not only the evolution of a species, but of one order (broader than family, genus, and species [used to name and distinguish organisms]) of animals into another. Who would doubt Darwin then?

The Red Cloud affair had already made O. C. Marsh, the bone hunter, a household name. Huxley had now helped establish him as America's champion of evolution.

In an ambitious and optimistic August 1877 speech for the American Association for the Advancement of Science, Marsh traced the line of vertebrates all the way from fish to humans. "To doubt evolution today," he told his audience, "is to doubt science, and science is only another name for truth."

When Darwin himself later reviewed Marsh's findings, he sent a letter:

My dear Professor Marsh,

I received some time ago your very kind note of July 28th, and yesterday the magnificent volume. I have looked with renewed admiration at the plates, and will soon read the text. Your work on these old birds, and on the many fossil animals of North America has afforded the best support to the theory of Evolution, which has appeared within the last twenty years. The general appearance of the copy which you have sent me is worthy of its contents, and I can say nothing stronger than this.

With cordial thanks, believe me,
Yours very sincerely,
Charles Darwin

COPE, WHO HAD APPLAUDED MARSH'S "DELIGHTFUL" BIRD WITH TEETH, WOULD always have mixed feelings about Darwin's theories—both for religious and scientific reasons. For him, natural selection had disturbing moral and social implications (for example, "survival of the fittest"). And from a scientific point of view, evolution just moved too slowly to be verified. Unlike Marsh, he was no politician. Though he could display great charm one-on-one, publicity was beyond him; his terse scientific papers lacked the drama of his private letters; he couldn't, or wouldn't, build an audience.

International renown from Darwin and his supporters made Marsh's reputation grow, as one peer put it, "very much more rapidly than that of Cope."

What was a mule head to do?

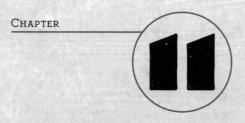

Obedient Servants

"We would be pleased to hear from you, as you are well known as an enthusiastic geologist and a man of means, both of which we are desirous of finding, more especially the latter."

—"HARLOW" AND "EDWARDS," IN A LETTER TO O. C. MARSH

By 1877, Cope and Marsh had been at odds for almost ten years, each a stinging insect to the other.

One of Marsh's assistants once overheard his boss, after reviewing a scientific paper by Cope, rattle the page and grump, "Gad! . . . *I wish the Lord would take him!*" Any competition or animosity the men felt toward one another could only grow, and it did, in leaps and bounds.

That year, a teacher, who also happened to be an amateur painter and bone hobbyist, was out fossil hunting with a friend near Morrison, Colorado, when he found what looked like a fossilized tree trunk in the Rocky Mountain

A Cope-sponsored dig site near Garden Park, Colorado, circa 1877.

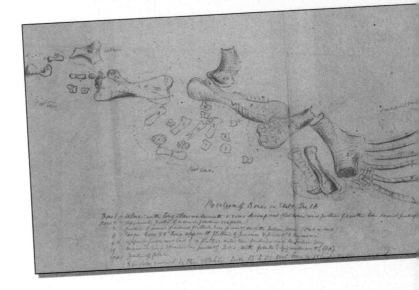

foothills. "It was so monstrous that I could hardly believe my eyes," Arthur Lakes wrote in his journal.

He supposed the fossil, at nearly three feet wide, might be a tremendous vertebra, a dinosaur's, but he needed an expert view.

He sent a sketch to Marsh at Yale, who offered to take a look if Lakes would forward samples. Lakes agreed and volunteered to locate more bones. Silence. He decided to try his luck with Cope, shipping bone samples to both paleontologists.

Marsh finally did respond with a $100 retainer for Lakes's services and, with it, his usual demands for discretion and secrecy. Unfortunately, Lakes owned up, Cope had already been notified, as had the press.

That got Marsh's attention. He telegrammed Benjamin Mudge with instructions to race to Morrison and secure the site.

"Satisfactory arrangements made for two months," Mudge wired back days later. "Jones cannot interfere."

"Jones," of course, was Cope. Marsh had established a code for communicating with his men in the field, and the word "Jones" was no doubt employed on a brisk basis.

Marsh also received corroboration from Mudge that the Morrison bones were *big*, "the very largest" Mudge had seen. They would turn out to belong to sauropods, a branch of plant-eating dinosaurs with long necks, the largest land animals ever to walk the earth.

But Marsh wasn't satisfied. He wanted even the bones that had gone to Cope. He pressured Lakes to recall them, and surprisingly, Cope let them go without a fight.

Mudge and Lakes set to digging. It wasn't easy work. The rock was unusually hard, the fossils easily damaged, but what fossils they were!

Marsh's first paper about Morrison,

THE MOTHER LODE OF JURASSIC MONSTERS

Made of sediments deposited during the late Jurassic period, the Morrison Formation would become a hotbed for dinosaur fossils in North America for nearly a decade. Scores of bone hunters worked there between 1877 and 1886.

Morrison yielded one magnificent beast after another—stegosaurs, apatosaurs, allosaurs, and more—producing some thousand crates of unprecedented material, all of which chugged its way back to New Haven, with similar bounty in Cope's Cañon City camp.

in which he described a Jurassic sauropod "quite distinct" from any yet described, naming it *Titanosaurus montanus* ("huge mountain lizard"), ran that July in an issue of *American Journal of Science*.

With a stroke of the pen, Marsh had replaced Cope's *Agathaumas* with the world's *new* largest known dinosaur.

He, by the by, also mentioned finding the bones of a *Laelaps*, the species Cope discovered in Haddonfield back in 1866. Marsh regretted to inform the scientific community that Cope had made an error while describing his first significant discovery: "This name *Laelaps* is preoccupied." It had been used in 1835 and again in 1843. "It may, therefore, be replaced," he pronounced, "by *Dryptosaurus* ['tearing lizard']."

Marsh wasn't out of line. The genus *Laelaps* had indeed been assigned already, to an arachnid. It was on the record, and that ruled it out scientifically. But the glee of being able to correct Cope in print, to undermine his rival's

A DINOSAUR BY ANY OTHER NAME

In zoology and paleontology, credit for a discovery doesn't always go to the individual (or group) who makes it. The first to formally "describe" the specimen wins the day—and the right to name the find.

The name selected can't have been used before. It must be unique in all the world, but how to keep track of all those names?

The system in use is based on the work of the eighteenth-century Swedish botanist Carl Linnaeus, who began to sort organisms into large groups called kingdoms. Today, living things are divided into five kingdoms: animals,

plants, fungi, protists, and monerans.

Kingdoms are made up of organisms that share basic characteristics but differ in other ways. Each kingdom can be divided into smaller and smaller groups, including phylum, class, order, family, genus, and—the smallest group—species.

In the Linnaeus system (and today's take on it: the International Code of Zoological Nomenclature), the first Latin word in an animal's or plant's scientific name, its genus, is capitalized and identifiable to scientists anywhere on the globe. The second, lowercased name is the animal's species name. Members of the same species share the same general

first proud find—that fearsome, eagle-taloned leaper—to the status of a mite, must have been great.

Cope, meanwhile, didn't mind relinquishing the Morrison bones. He had a secret.

Another schoolteacher and fossil hobbyist in Colorado, O. W. Lucas, had run across big bones in March and notified the academy.

Cope dubbed the new find, a massive sauropod, *Camarasaurus* ("chambered lizard"). The jury was out on the total dimensions of the beast, Cope announced in his description, but "this remarkable creature . . . exceeds in its proportions any other land animal hitherto discovered." Lest there be doubt, Cope went on, adding for good measure: "including the one found . . . by Professor Lakes."

Furious, Marsh dispatched Mudge to Cañon City.

The spy had to admit that Cope's fossils were big, bigger than theirs. What's more, physical appearance and can reproduce together.

Some names are descriptive, others nod to mythological characters, and still others, like *Hadrosaurus foulkii*, honor the person who physically made the discovery.

In the 1870s, the quickest way to publish a scientific description was to send a brief, dated letter or telegram to an industry journal. Announcements were printed up and often circulated separately from the magazine and mailed out to subscribers. Societies also included "separates" in their meeting notes, another way of getting a discovery into the official record. In a dispute, the date on which a scientific paper or "separate" was received, printed, or read aloud determined "priority."

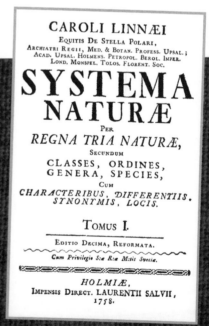

Title page of Carl Linnaeus's
Systema Naturae, *1758.*

because they had been housed in softer rock, the bones were in superior condition. Marsh's men had to use dynamite at times to get at their bones, while Cope's crew got by with picks.

Mudge managed to locate a bone bed nearby and appease his boss.

"Secure all possible," Marsh commanded. "Jones has violated all agreements."

IN AUGUST, MARSH'S MEN DUG UP A SEVENTY-FIVE-FOOT BEAST HE NAMED *Apatosaurus* ("deceptive lizard") and described as the world's *longest* land dinosaur (so far).

Cope's Cañon City crew soon located one he dubbed *Amphicoelias* ("double hollowed"): the world's *tallest* dinosaur (so far).

Marsh's team came back with one of the *weirdest* dinosaurs (so far)—the bony-plated, spiky-tailed *Stegosaurus* ("roofed lizard").

And so it went, volley after volley.

When he received a letter from two shadowy Wyoming men who claimed to have their hands on fossil bones bigger than any in Colorado, Marsh wired for samples and dispatched Williston to Wyoming.

The dealers, billing themselves as Harlow and Edwards (Marsh called them "Obedient Servants"), were in fact William Harlow Reed and Will Edwards Carlin, employees at a tiny railroad station in Como Bluff, Wyoming.

Williston took one look—the site was brimming with fossils—and informed Marsh that the specimens there beat out Cañon City and Morrison hands down in terms of "perfection, accessibility, and quantity." But there would be steep competition. A Harvard scout had been seen nosing around. Someone had informed the Smithsonian of the cache. The Smithsonian signaled Cope.

Marsh paid Carlin and Reed (more than he would have liked) to dig discreetly (and *now*) to beat the odds.

The two men—Reed more enthusiastically than Carlin—endured subzero temperatures and violent winds that winter, carting bones as thick as tree trunks from the bluff to the station with raw hands, crating them, loading them onto trains, and shipping them to New Haven.

Marsh opened one shipment after another, delighted to name species after new species—*Diplodocus*, *Allosaurus*, and many more—and write up his research at breakneck speed.

In April 1878 word of Marsh's doings—and of the "riches" for the taking at Como Bluff—appeared in Wyoming's *Laramie Daily Sentinel*. Carlin had leaked the news, Marsh deduced. He sent his loyal man Williston to silence his "Obedient Servant" and to stand ground if Cope turned up.

Williston, who must have seen spies everywhere under Marsh's dictate, sent word of a stranger in town named Haines. "There is no doubt that he is direct from Cope," Williston told his boss. "[He] didn't mention Cope's name, but yours frequently, *rather* disparagingly!"

Summer came and went, with no additional signs of the Philadelphian in Como Bluff.

Marsh looked for other ways to sideline his opponent.

An interesting conversation was under way in Washington, DC, that summer. Congress hoped to merge the various US geological surveys into one: four surveys led to overlap and confusion, many argued, and cost too much.

Marsh was serving as vice president of the National Academy of Sciences at the time (later, in 1883, he would be elected NAS president, holding the post for a dozen years) and used his clout to lobby in favor. He advised a single government survey and a streamlined staff, including, not coincidentally, a chief paleontologist. Who better for the job, his supporters proposed, than Marsh himself?

When he heard, Cope was stunned. The surveys had paid for his fossil collection and published several of his discoveries. He was even now wrapping up an ambitious book of paleontology that would, he'd long assumed, print at government expense. After all, he compiled most of his research with the Hayden survey.

If Marsh was named chief paleontologist of a lone survey, it would leave Cope entirely vulnerable. The government (and Marsh, Cope feared) would monopolize resources and shut him out of the fossil market. A move like this could spell the end of his career in paleontology.

He called on sympathetic colleagues to argue against the ruling, but on March 21, 1879, Congress opted for a single survey, the US Geological Survey.

Seething with anger and resentment, Cope turned to Como Bluff for revenge.

Marsh got the news later that spring: Carlin was now shipping fossils to Cope! As Como Bluff stationmaster, Carlin wouldn't even let Reed crate Marsh's fossils inside the station freight room but forced his one-time workmate to labor out on the windy platform and pitch camp in a quarry. Not exactly an "Obedient Servant."

William Harlow Reed, circa 1879.

With the mutinous Carlin digging for Cope—and Reed for Marsh—the former partners went to absurd lengths to safeguard their digs. Neither let the other in range of a work site. They pitched tents over their trenches to hide the goods (also a handy shield against bad weather).

When strangers lurked near one

of his digs, Reed, in buckskin fringes, climbed a bluff and rained dirt and rocks down on them.

Marsh visited Como Bluff in June, checking in on a number of active dig sites and urging his men to produce more bones more quickly. But he also entertained Lakes after supper with tales of his Fort Bridger expedition. The men enjoyed lunch the next day at a reputed train robber's hideout. Marsh, in his derby hat, posed with another bone hunter while Lakes immortalized the scene in watercolor.

Arthur Lakes's painting of an afternoon spent idling with O. C. Marsh.

Cope came to call at Como Bluff, too, spending two days there in August. In a letter to Julia, he reported: "[T]he boys have dug up a huge, flesh-eating saurian which they will send off in the morning." The fossil proved to be one of the most intact *Allosaurus* skeletons yet found.

In that brief window, Cope also charmed Lakes, who described the enemy

Excavation of the dinosaur Diplodocus.

in his journals as a "tall, rather interesting-looking young man." Cope could as easily converse about Lakes's native England as about geology, it seems, and he kept the group in stitches "by singing comic songs with a refrain at the end like the howl of a coyote."

To Marsh, Lakes wrote, "The *Monstrum horrendum* Cope has been and gone, and I must say that what I saw of him I liked very much, his manner is so affable and his conversation very agreeable." Aware that his reader might disapprove of his approval, Lakes added, "I only wish I could feel sure he had a sound reputation for honesty."

After four active seasons in Quarry 10, one of Morrison's best, Marsh's man Reed took "the liberty to demolish" leftover fossils so "Jones" and other competitors couldn't benefit from them.

Cope hurried to print his findings in academic journals and even bought up the esteemed *The American Naturalist* as a vehicle for his own writing. Always quick to the pen, he was unstoppable now, and would ultimately become one of the most prolific authors in the history of science in the United States.

Marsh objected as strenuously as ever to Cope's hasty work—and the mistakes it introduced into the literature—but his own efforts could be just as rushed. He would publish some fifty-five papers describing his gigantic finds.

Marsh's Como Bluff work continued till 1889, overlapping with equally impressive digs in a late Cretaceous deposit between 1888 and 1892.

As the "Bone Rush" or "Bone Wars" continued in the West, Cope and Marsh escalated their personal attacks. No amount of success or fame, and no discovery, however massive, could distract from their monumental hatred for one another.

SCIENTISTS WAGE BITTER WARFARE.

Prof. Cope, of the University of Pennsylvania, Brings Serious Charges Against Director Powell and Prof. Marsh, of the Geological Survey.

CORROBORATION IN PLENTY.

Learned Men Come to the Pennsylvanian's Support with Allegations of Ignorance, Plagiarism and Incompetence Against the Accused Officials.

IMPORTANT COLLATERAL ISSUE.

The National Academy of Sciences, of Which Professor Marsh is President, is Charged with Being Packed in the Interests of the Survey.

RED HOT DENIALS PUT FORTH.

Heavy Blows Dealt in Attack and Defence and Lots of Hard Nuts Provided for Scientific Digestion.

WILL CONGRESS INVESTIGATE?

PROFESSOR COPE.

12

Scientific Smackdown

> *"To meet these charges one and all is an easy task, but not a pleasant one, as I shall have to use plain words."*
>
> —O. C. MARSH

B y the summer season of 1881, the word was out, the market in Colorado and Wyoming was booming, and Como Bluff was bustling with bone hunters amateur and otherwise.

Back east, Marsh and Cope were so inundated with bones, they couldn't open all the boxes; they certainly didn't have time to describe all these fossil riches or ponder their paleontological significance.

When they did delve in, as Marsh did in restoring his first dinosaur, piecing together the skeleton using head, tail, and some limb bones from other sites, the race for priority again led to sloppy work.

Marsh lost first Lakes and then Reed due to the squabbles, intrigue, and low pay. As the game of musical workers continued, he was named chief

Headlines!

paleontologist by the new US Geological Survey (USGS) led by John Wesley Powell, an expected appointment that gave Marsh an ample salary, federal funding for research, a staff, and the power to force his rival out of the game, isolating Cope and draining his government funding.

Iconic Brontosaurus *in advertising.*

TRACKING *BRONTOSAURUS*

In 1877, O. C. Marsh described a new species of sauropod dinosaur from an incomplete skeleton, as paleontologists often do, naming it *Apatosaurus ajax* ("deceptive lizard"). Two years later, he named another sauropod from scant material: *Brontosaurus excelsus* ("thunder lizard"), believing the specimen was similar but distinct enough from *Apatosaurus* to warrant a new genus name. When he got his hands on more bones in 1883, Marsh did a full reconstruction, ending up with one of the most complete sauropods on record, sans skull.

But *Brontosaurus*, some would argue, never existed.

In 1903, paleontologist Elmer Riggs compared the bones of both *Brontosaurus* and *Apatosaurus*. They came from creatures similar enough to share a genus, he proposed, and since *Apatosaurus* had been named first, that name took priority.

Brontosaurus excelsus became *Apatosaurus excelsus*, and most scientists agreed that *Brontosaurus* was no longer a valid scientific name.

So why did it persist for another eighty years? Why did *Brontosaurus* go on to

Panicked, Cope invested most of what remained of his inheritance—and he had already spent much on expeditions and fossils—in a New Mexico silver mine, a miscalculation that nearly ruined him. He simply couldn't compete with Marsh anymore, and by the mid-1880s he was nearly broke. Though it must have riled him to give up his independence, especially on Marsh's account, Cope applied for positions at the Smithsonian, the American Museum of Natural History, Princeton University, and elsewhere, but his reputation for being brash and combative preceded him.

He continued work on his huge book, *The Vertebrata of the Tertiary Formations of the West*—or "Cope's Bible," as it would be called—some thousand pages of text with seventy-five detailed illustrations. It would be the first of two volumes, his life's work, but Cope couldn't get volume two published. He couldn't afford to. He repeatedly requested funding from the USGS to do so,

become one of the most beloved icons of all time, making its lumbering appearance on product packaging, cartoons like *The Flintstones*, and, as recently as 1989, a US postage stamp?

The material Marsh used to describe *Brontosaurus* was kept at Yale. He never made an effort to publicly display the partial skeleton his crew unearthed at Como Bluff. But in 1905, when the American Museum of Natural History (AMNH) put a reconstruction on exhibit, it was, for much of the public, the first unforgettable glimpse of these giants. Though familiar with Riggs's research, AMNH's Henry Fairfield Osborn chose to label the mount *Brontosaurus*, cementing that name in the public consciousness.

To Riggs's frustration, the crowd-pleasing dinosaur went right on being promoted with the wrong name, not only in New York City but at the Carnegie Museum of Natural History in Pittsburgh and the Field Museum in Chicago. When the animal's missing skull was located later, the name *Apatosaurus* finally began to gain in popularity, at least among scientists.

But then, a trio of scientists sat down to examine nearly every known specimen of "diplodocid" sauropod. Under their criteria, some species of *Apatosaurus*, including *Apatosaurus excelsus*, were distinct enough to warrant a new genus name.

One just happened to be handy and available—*Brontosaurus*!—good news for Thunder Lizard fans everywhere.

"MARSHIANA"

All but forced out of the paleontology game, Cope appealed to Congress in 1885, and to Powell's political enemies in Washington, DC. When he found no help there, he turned his rage back to its source. Notoriously stingy with staff and students, Marsh didn't allow his assistants to publish independent findings; he didn't credit them in publications they had contributed to; he paid them far too little and valued them less. Cope met behind closed doors with several ambitious young men in—or formerly in—Marsh's employ, heard their complaints, soothed and sympathized, and scribbled out pages of testimony. His "Marshiana," as he called it, was a curious collection in its own right, and Cope supported it as compulsively as any other.

but Powell, the new head of the survey, was a Marsh sympathizer—and blocking publication of Cope's work gave Marsh time to air his own findings—so he refused.

In 1888, to keep afloat financially, Cope borrowed from friends and took out loans. He tried and failed to sell some of his fossils at fair prices, meanwhile viciously stepping up his attack on the man he held responsible for his plight. When Marsh ran for reelection as president of NAS (a post he held from 1883 to 1895), Cope's mean-spirited campaign shocked his peers. They might not have liked Marsh—many people didn't—but they liked Cope's bad behavior less. Marsh was a competent leader, and the membership voted him back without a fuss.

In 1889, Cope's luck finally turned a little. The University of Pennsylvania offered him a position as a geology professor. But his relief wouldn't last.

In December, he received a fateful letter from the US secretary of the interior, a demand that Cope surrender his fossil collection—gathered during his time with the Hayden survey—to the national museum.

His beloved mountain of bones was now government property.

Cope was stunned, terrified, and furious. Without his fossils, what did he have? He had already lost his fortune. In 1890, he was so hard up for money he had to rent out both of his houses and live jammed in with his family, his pets—a land tortoise from Florida who roamed the floors and a Gila monster in a glass tank—and, of course, his mountain of fossils in a tiny apartment in Philadelphia. He'd spent a fair amount of his own money on his world-class collection and had the receipts to prove it. The claim was preposterous, no doubt precipitated by Marsh and Powell, and he wouldn't have it.

What's more, he wanted revenge.

Cope brought his complaints and his Marsh dossier to the press. An unscrupulous reporter was only too happy to peddle Cope's "Marshiana" to the *New York Herald* and land a series. The public had followed the "gold rush" enthusiastically, and scientific fisticuffs might just rival the popular round-the-world exploits of the *New York World*'s Nellie Bly.

The January 12, 1890, headline shouted:

SCIENTISTS WAGE BITTER WARFARE
PROF. COPE OF THE UNIVERSITY OF PENN-SYLVANIA BRINGS SERIOUS CHARGES AGAINST DIRECTOR POWELL AND PROF. MARSH OF THE GEO-LOGICAL SURVEY

He was making those claims—that Marsh had gained his USGS job through political wheeling and dealing with friends and associates; that the Yale professor wasn't fit to lead the NAS; that his papers were full of errors; that he rarely did any research himself or credited staff who did; that he outright took credit for other scientists' work—because the government had demanded he release his valuable collection, fossils meticulously acquired and prepared over decades.

As for Powell and USGS, they were guilty of misuse of government funds, corruption, and incompetence. Cope cited a "gigantic politico-scientific monopoly." The government machine had shut him out of the field he had devoted his life to. They had shut out *any* competition.

Cope reveled in his attack, telling a friend, "Either [Marsh] or I must go under. . . . I have, I believe, performed an unpleasant but necessary duty to my country."

To stir the pot (and avoid being sued), the *Herald* had sent copies of the edition to Marsh and Powell, inviting comment.

Powell lashed back first. Cope was driven by "great vanity." He was "jealous and suspicious," unable to "associate on terms of cooperation."

Marsh's reply took a week and filled an entire page with vitriol. Cope was inept, a liar, a thief. The affronted professor from Yale listed Cope's sins, one by one, in grim detail. The Philadelphian had visited Yale and lifted research; he had spied in Wyoming—and let's not forget 1869 and the *Elasmosaurus* debacle: Cope put his head on backward!

"Has Professor Cope since learned wisdom from his increasing years?" Marsh mused. "The public must judge. The scientific world has long since passed judgment."

Laymen enjoyed the blood sport for a time, but the scientific community was, again, disturbed and disappointed. The scandal occupied the press for two weeks but soon lost steam, though Cope gained sympathy. The government dropped its demands and let him keep his fossil collection.

After a subsequent congressional hearing in 1892, Powell resigned. Marsh was roundly dismissed from his chiefdom (he spiraled into the same financial straits as Cope, Yale salary notwithstanding), and the department of paleontology was eliminated. A quarter of the survey's funding was slashed—bad news for bone diggers.

In a last delicious blow for Cope, the government recalled any items from Marsh's personal collection that had been acquired with federal funding: the lucky Smithsonian inherited eighty tons of Marsh fossils.

With their finances and reputations in ruin, both scientists slipped into decline.

In 1894 Cope's beloved daughter, Julia, left home to marry. Cope and Annie moved to Haverford to stay close, but the plan collapsed, and Cope found himself alone.

Annie "left him," his friend Osborn told a correspondent later, "largely for financial reasons" but also because, at long last, she had found it "too hard to live with a genius."

Cope was a popular teacher and lecturer and kept up a brisk writing schedule, but his many (and ignored) health issues caught up with him in April 1897. He died at age fifty-six, surrounded by his fossils—with the last word and little else, it would seem. His personal losses rippled out to science. Though wonders were yet to come, with survey funds cut, paleontology lost much of its government funding, and the study of fossils slacked off.

Marsh finished his career at Yale and turned over his vast collections to the university in 1898. He died just two years after his nemesis, of pneumonia, at age sixty-seven, with $186 in his bank account. His tombstone reads, "To Yale he gave his collections, his services, and his estate."

Cope's cluttered study, circa 1897, near the end of his life.

Allosaurus,
a large carnivore.

Do we know whether
Allosaurus ate Apatosaurus?

Endnote

"Sleeping on a dragon's hoard with greedy,
dragonish thoughts in his heart, he had
become a dragon himself."

—C. S. LEWIS, *THE VOYAGE OF THE DAWN TREADER*

C ope and Marsh never lived to see the degree to which their life's labor—
and joint obsession—would make its mark on the world.

Highlights from their precious collections would be bought up, recalled, shuffled, restored, and mounted by other professionals. Skeletons harvested over three decades were erected in museum galleries in New York,
New Haven, Pittsburgh, and Washington, inspiring other bone rushes, other
rivalries. Dinosaur fossils, which some early humans mistook for dragon
bones, would stand tall—suspended as if by magic—in gallery after echoing
gallery, delighting curious minds around the world.

Resurrected, these beasts of old fired millions of imaginations, locking the
prehistoric past in focus, just as Cope had once done while re-creating vanished
ecosystems—long-necked creatures lumbering in swamps, skies a-*swoosh*
with leathery wings—for friends and family around the supper table.

Between them, if not exactly together, Marsh and Cope described 132

*A nearly complete Allosaurus skeleton unearthed by Cope's team at Como Bluff in 1879
and not unpacked until after his death.*

dinosaur species (the actual number of new discoveries shrank as later researchers merged or purged duplicate finds), paving the way for generations of paleontologists and forever fixing the "terrible lizard" in the hearts and minds of the public.

Cope's rangy genius had added some 1,400 papers and several books—including his "Bible," *Vertebrata*, and key research on reptiles and amphibians—to the scientific literature. Marsh's ancient horse fossils became a symbol of evolutionary progress. His birds with teeth helped prove that modern birds descended from dinosaurs.

But in their lifetimes, during the bone rush that consumed them, their race became its own destination. Though each had set out in the pioneering spirit of discovery, the rush of acquiring and the ruthless need to surpass the other trumped all else, and like the mythological dragon hoarding treasure for treasure's sake, ever guarding its lair and its advantage, they were blinded by greed.

"Marsh was never to have fossils 'enough,'" wrote one contemporary. "Even with almost every box opened at the Museum yielding a new species, or throwing new light on an old one, he saw need for more and yet more material."

Cope was no different. During an 1878 European trip, he paid $2,500 for a collection of Argentinean mammal fossils. Because they were of groups distinct to South America, these turned out to be hugely significant when the American Museum of Natural History acquired them in 1897. But Cope never found time to describe them. The boxes housing the collection were only partly opened, and, overshadowed by the continual flow of specimens from all over the United States, many remained still unopened until after he died. Cope never fully understood what he had.

From greed sprang selfishness. Just as they failed to do justice to the material they helped discover, to give it meaning and context, Cope and Marsh failed to nurture a new generation of paleontologists (and Marsh outright discouraged younger scientists). Seen as ruthless and petty, an embarrassing spectacle of ambition run amok, the Cope-Marsh feud built a climate of mistrust among fellow scientists and blemished the scientific reputation of the United States for decades.

It's true that Cope and Marsh were products of their time. Like the robber barons who dominated industry, finance, and other fields in the Gilded Age, they had to compete to survive, or at least to stay on top, as Joseph Leidy's fall from prominence proved. The American West was seen as a place where rugged individuals triumphed, adventure and fortune-making went hand in hand, and greed and progress—at any cost—ruled the day. The race to build the railroads and the attack on the Plains Indians' way of life, including the near-destruction of the bison, are fierce reminders of the dark side of such ambition.

EARLIER IN THE SAME CENTURY, ACROSS THE ATLANTIC, CHARLES DARWIN AND the coauthor of his theory, Alfred Russel Wallace, found themselves—like Marsh and Cope—in the awkward position of "discovering" the same treasure around the same time.

They didn't realize it at first, but both men had conceived of natural selection, Darwin as early as the 1830s, holding back his research for two decades out of fear.

Wallace spent years in Southeast Asia, studying and collecting animal and plant specimens, and was an outsider. Unlike Darwin, he had no money and no social standing. He left school at age fourteen and made his living selling insect specimens to museums and collectors.

While exploring the wildlife of South America and Asia, Wallace had sometimes supplied Darwin with birds for his studies. He got up the courage to ask for the older scientist's help in publishing his ideas on evolution. When he sent his theory in 1858, Darwin was first stunned and then stricken with despair, fearing Wallace would be the first to claim credit for the idea.

Friends of Darwin's arranged to present papers by both men at London's Linnean Society in 1858, where the theory didn't make much of a stir. Darwin seized the chance to rush publication of *On the Origin of Species*, which not only became a bestseller in 1859 but one of the most influential scientific books of all time. Wallace, it seems, went about his travels and turned to the study of biogeography.

Was he peeved that Darwin got all the credit? The two men had become "work friends," a bit like Marsh and Cope originally were, if not close. Wallace admired Darwin and never expressed bitterness toward him. He seemed honored to be accepted as a "junior" partner in such important work. Many minds had contributed already, and many more would weigh in before the theory took hold, but the combined efforts of two men at a crossroads put something very big in motion.

What if, instead of working together, they had resorted to spying, sabotage, and destruction of scientific evidence?

The "Great Bone Wars," or the "Great Bone Rush," will live long in paleontological folklore. It's a good yarn, as Buffalo Bill might say. But it's worth wondering what might have surfaced if these two great minds had worked together, if competition and cooperation served the same end.

What's funny is that Marsh and Cope, who hated each other with such energy—who spent most of their professional lives trying to outdo, outthink, outpace, and outdistance one another—are almost never mentioned individually. It's the *feud* people remember. Theirs is a shared legacy, and history had the last word.

Dinosaur Hunting in the United States

EASTERN STATES

Because many nineteenth-century paleontologists (including Cope and Marsh) hailed from the east, an impressive array of western fossils landed in eastern collections.

Smithsonian National Museum of Natural History

WASHINGTON, DC

https://naturalhistory.si.edu

American Museum of Natural History

NEW YORK, NY

https://www.amnh.org

Yale Peabody Museum of Natural History

NEW HAVEN, CT

http://peabody.yale.edu

The Academy of Natural Sciences of Drexel University

PHILADELPHIA, PA

http://www.ansp.org

Carnegie Museum of Natural History

PITTSBURGH, PA

https://carnegiemnh.org

Beneski Museum of Natural History at Amherst College

AMHERST, MA

https://www.amherst.edu/museums /naturalhistory

MIDWESTERN STATES

Field Museum

CHICAGO, IL

https://www.fieldmuseum.org

Cleveland Museum of Natural History

CLEVELAND, OH

https://www.cmnh.org

WESTERN STATES

The Montana Dinosaur Trail

A dozen-plus statewide exhibits linked by a map and a "prehistoric passport"

www.mtdinotrail.org

Museum of the Rockies

BOZEMAN, MT

https://museumoftherockies.org

Garden Park Fossil Area

NORTH OF CAÑON CITY, CO

http://www.handsontheland.org/garden-park

Dinosaur National Monument

CO/UT

https://www.nps.gov/dino/index.htm

Denver Museum of Nature and Science

DENVER, CO

http://www.dmns.org

Morrison Natural History Museum

MORRISON, CO

http://www.mnhm.org

Dinosaur Ridge

MORRISON, CO

http://www.dinoridge.org/index.html

The Wyoming Dinosaur Center

THERMOPOLIS, WY

http://www.wyodino.org

Fossil Cabin

MEDICINE BOW, WY

https://www.wyohistory.org/encyclopedia/fossil-cabin

Natural History Museum of Los Angeles County

LOS ANGELES, CA

https://nhm.org/site

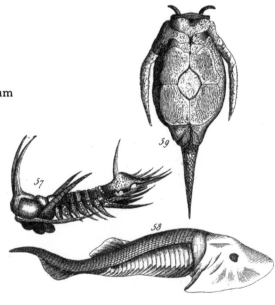

Source Notes

THE TERRIBLE LIZARD OF NEW JERSEY

"the minds of the masses . . . advance science": *The Gilded Dinosaur* by Mark Jaffe, p. 11.

"many accidents . . . destruction of property.": *Proceedings of the Academy of Natural Sciences of Philadelphia*, Volume 21, p. 235.

1: THE PRODIGY

"I am not constructed . . . general run of people.": Jaffe, p. 48.

"Pigs have bristles . . . Snakes are bare.": *Biographical Memoir of Edward Drinker Cope, 1840–1897* by Henry Fairfield Osborn, p. 130.

"incessant activity" . . . "Master Davis": *The Bonehunters' Revenge* by David Rains Wallace, pp. 15–16.

"Work, work, work . . . fancy for it.": Jaffe, p. 45.

"admiration of nature . . . 'investigation.'": *Impressions of Great Naturalists* by Henry Fairfield Osborn, p. 173.

"A public disgrace . . . willful disorder.": Jaffe, p. 45.

"wicked boy . . . bad conduct number": Wallace, p. 17.

"I am sure . . . teacher and myself.": Jaffe, p. 45.

great independence . . . action: Osborn, p. 170.

"The whole ground is gone over . . . a few weeds": Wallace, p. 17.

"He does things in an unnecessarily offensive manner.": Jaffe, p. 50.

"I have very interesting times . . . every second.": *Battle of the Dinosaur Bones* by Rebecca L. Johnson, p. 11.

"sensibilities scorched into a crust . . . painful thoughts": Jaffe, p. 47.

"If I know myself . . . do not much doubt, in insanity.": Wallace, p. 20.

"Professor Cope called upon me . . . willing to be his friend.": Jaffe, pp. 47–48.

"an amiable woman . . . frivolity.": Wallace, p. 21.

"As I have learned . . . trouble herself.": Jaffe, p. 49.

DREAMING OF STRANGE FORMS

so revolted . . . "melancholy": *Joseph Leidy: The Last Man Who Knew Everything* by Leonard Warren, p. 27.

"You can have no idea . . . eyes in them.": Wallace, p. 48.

2: THE PROFESSOR

"I changed my mind . . . really study.": Wallace, p. 26.

"good natural abilities . . . hardly formed and developed": Wallace, p. 25.

"little impression" . . . "shrewd with a touch of cunning in it": Wallace, p. 26.

Daddy . . . Captain: Wallace, p. 27.

"Libby . . . things.": Jaffe, p. 28.

"He was always very odd . . . acquainted with him.": Wallace, p. 27.

"munificent donation": Wallace, p. 29.

LIKE CONFESSING A MURDER

not apt to follow blindly the lead of other men: *Charles Darwin: An Anthology* edited by Marston Bates and Philip S. Humphrey, p. 31.

It is like confessing a murder: http://www.lettersofnote.com/2009/09/it-is-like -confessing-murder.html.

3: A THEFT

"I took him through New Jersey . . . for money.": Wallace, p. 41.

valuable illustrations of palaeontology and geology . . . cabinet of the Academy.: *The Dinosaur Papers: 1676–1906,* by David B. Weishampel and Nadine M. White, p. 263.

"I thought best . . . dinosaurian.": Wallace, p. 40.

"a cross . . . claw of a lion": Jaffe, p. 10.

"probably of Buckland's genus . . . I have yet made.": Wallace, p. 40.

"Flummery there is . . . scientific work.": Wallace, p. 41.

"After the work of the winter . . . three new species of Saurians.": Wallace, p. 41.

4: AN "ABOMINABLE VOLUME" AND A HAT FULL OF BONES

"My own life work seemed laid out before me.": Wallace, p. 53.

"The most inviting . . . regions of the west" . . . "Certainly in no other country . . . charged with fossils.": Jaffe, p. 25.

"new and strange . . . eye could see": Jaffe, p. 26.

"undoubtedly human": Wallace, p. 52.

"I was eager . . . good friends.": Jaffe, p. 26.

"I showed them to my fellow travelers . . . this new field.": Wallace, p. 53.

"During his life . . . three toes.": Jaffe, p. 27.

"new and gigantic . . . New Jersey" . . . "the one that got away.": Jaffe, p. 12.

MISSING PROOF

abominable volume: http://darwin-online.org.uk/content/frameset?keywords=volume%20abominable&pageseq=184&itemID=F1452.2&viewtype=text (p. 168)

5: A MISTAKE

"[Cope's] wounded vanity . . . my bitter enemy.": Wallace, p. 42.

"well calculated . . . general public.": Jaffe, p. 6.

"I noticed that the articulations . . . one end from another.": Wallace, p. 42.

"[I] retained . . . hard to bear.": Wallace, p. 39.

READING THE BONES

"I found myself as if placed . . . resumed its place.": Wallace, p. 36.

THE JOLLY OLD BEAST IS NOT DECEASED

"The jolly old beast / Is not deceased. / There's life in him
   again! / ROAR!": http://www.cam.ac.uk/research/features
   /iggy-the-iguanodon-and-the-160-year-old-dinosaur-song.

ALL THIS THING CALLED SCIENCE

"I am tired . . . all such things?": Jaffe, p. 4.

6: THIS COUNTRY OF BIG THINGS

As night closed over our geologists . . . more than science: "The Yale College
   Expedition of 1870" by C. W. Betts, *Harper's New Monthly Magazine*,
   p. 664.

in a state of unusual excitement: *Harper's*, p. 663.

a matter of hourly apprehension: *Harper's*, p. 665.

mounted on Indian ponies, and armed . . . bowie-knife: *Harper's*, p. 663.

had to thank a thunder-shower . . . spoiled it all!: *Harper's*, p. 664.

"an outdoor man . . . appreciated art": Wallace, p. 59.

mighty changes of geology . . . "you know how it is yourself, Bill!": *Harper's*, p. 664.

burned prairie . . . dead grasshoppers: *Harper's*, p. 666.

old-time trappers clad in buckskin: Jaffe, p. 35.

for his lady-love: *Harper's*, p. 666.

"Father! . . . tired of talking.": *Iron Rails, Iron Men, and the Race to Link the Nation* by
   Martin W. Sandler, p. 39.

"the brink of a vast basin . . . ruins of the world.": Wallace, p. 62.

more disappointed . . . illness or accident: *Harper's*, p. 671.

"market for fossil vertebrates . . . that market.": Wallace, p. 64.

"made a careful calculation . . . twenty feet": Wallace, p. 63.

"truly . . . country of big things.": Jaffe, p. 53.

WHERE THE BUFFALO ROAMED

"wonderful . . . R.R. track": Wallace, p. 71.

"Day after day . . . masses of flames.": Jaffe, p. 68.

"Have the white men become children . . . eat?": *Our Hearts Fell to the Ground* by Colin G. Calloway, p. 123.

7: HI TONED FOR A BONE SHARP

"You will see therefore . . . a necessity.": Jaffe, p. 71.

"The stories I hear . . . are not bad.": Wallace, p. 72.

"I asked [Cope] not to go into that field . . . You can sympathize.": http://enacademic .com/dic.nsf/enwiki/565381.

"good bone contry . . . for a bone sharp": Wallace, p. 81.

GRUDGING INSPIRATION

"of the wonderful animals . . . entranced.": Wallace, p. 74.

"I listened with rapt attention . . . into an ancient world.": *Charles R. Knight: Autobiography of an Artist* by Charles Robert Knight, p. 75.

8: HYDRA-HEADED

"I was never so angry in my life.": Jaffe, p. 91.

"The broad valley . . . with buffalo" . . . "in the exact manner . . . had taught me": Jaffe, p. 78.

"close up the expedition . . . coyotes": Jaffe, p. 82.

"very weak & helpless": Jaffe, p. 83.

"your bird with teeth . . . I was never so angry in my life.": Jaffe, p. 91.

"I feel I have been deeply wronged . . . no longer a virtue.": Jaffe, p. 92.

"[Marsh] seems hot on the path of . . . for one person?": Jaffe, p. 86.

"Prof. Cope . . . observations": Wallace, p. 88.

"Marsh has always been . . . into insanity.": Jaffe, p. 94.

"We regret . . . space to its consideration.": Jaffe, p. 97.

"Prof. Cope's errors . . . ungracious task.": Wallace, p. 90.

"Formerly, every fossil . . . I cannot compete.": *The Bone Hunters* by Url Lanham, p. 18.

9: WARINESS AND CONTROVERSY

"I wish they would stop . . . *name* a hundred.": Jaffe, p. 107.

"My time is too fully occupied . . . before the public.": Wallace, p. 90.

"I have been . . . they were.": Jaffe, p. 107.

"simple justice.": Jaffe, p. 106.

"mule head": Jaffe, p. 95.

He Who Picks Up Stones Running: Jaffe, p. 25.

"rare specimens . . . and named.": Wallace, p. 99.

"I put my soul in the letter . . . my own expense" . . . "Go to work.": Jaffe, pp. 166–67.

"The professor was strongly advised . . . death on the other tribe.": Jaffe, p. 173.

"attacks of fever": Wallace, p. 155.

"was so weak . . . side when he walked.": Wallace, p. 123.

"typical frontier town . . . whiskey for sale.": Jaffe, p. 172.

"Everyone considers . . . to which I am going.": Jaffe, p. 176.

"the best I ever had": Wallace, p. 126.

"splendid grass . . . do not know.": Wallace, p. 124.

"they were greatly amused . . . put them back in.": Jaffe, p. 177.

"not worth digging out.": Wallace, p. 124.

"that dinosaurs . . . immense size": Wallace, p. 125.

"I have never known . . . will's power over the body.": Wallace, p. 126.

"The lands are . . . injured himself.": Jaffe, p. 179.

ALL KINDS OF BEINGS WERE CHANGED TO STONE

"All kinds of beings . . . live no longer.": *Fossil Legends of the First Americans* by Adrienne Mayor, p. 106.

BIG BONE CHIEF

Big Bone Chief: Jaffe, p. 122.

"He told the . . . best white man I ever saw.": Jaffe, p. 143.

10: ANOTHER NAME FOR TRUTH

Another Name for Truth: "Introduction and Succession of Vertebrate Life in America," by O. C. Marsh, introductory page.

"No collection . . . evidence.": Jaffe, p. 157.

"We are up to our knees . . . mud": Jaffe, p. 164.

"My excellent host . . . as if I were in my own house.": Wallace, p. 134.

"[Marsh] is a wonderfully good fellow . . . wonderful thing I ever saw.": Wallace, p. 134.

"My own explorations . . . New World, not the Old.": Jaffe, p. 156.

"I believe you are a magician . . . conjure up.": Jaffe, p. 157.

"Seldom has prophecy . . . West.": Wallace, p. 136.

"I am thinking of discoursing . . . contents of those boxes.": Jaffe, p. 163.

"To doubt evolution . . . name for truth.": Wallace, p. 138.

"My dear Professor Marsh . . . sincerely, Charles Darwin": *The Life and Letters of Charles Darwin* edited by Francis Darwin, pp. 417–18.

"very much more rapidly . . . Cope.": Wallace, p. 139.

DARWIN'S BULLDOG

Is man an ape or an angel? . . . new-fangled theories.: Benjamin Disraeli, speech at Oxford Diocesan Conference (November 25, 1864). https://en.wikiquote.org/wiki/Benjamin_Disraeli.

"I finished your book . . . beak in readiness.": https://www.darwinproject.ac.uk /letter/DCP-LETT-2544.xml.

"What is the good of my writing a thundering big book . . . for its size?": Jaffe, p. 146.

guide, philosopher, and friend . . . my life work. "Thomas Henry Huxley" by O. C. Marsh, p. 177.

11: OBEDIENT SERVANTS

"We would be pleased to hear . . . especially the latter.": Wallace, p. 148.

"Gad! . . . *I wish the Lord would take him!*": Wallace, p. 143.

"It was so monstrous that I could hardly believe my eyes . . . the very largest": Wallace, p. 145.

"quite distinct": Johnson, p. 40.

"This name *Laelaps* . . . *Dryptosaurus.*": Johnson, p. 41.

"This remarkable creature . . . Professor Lakes" . . . "Secure all possible . . . all agreements.": Wallace, p. 147.

Obedient Servants: Jaffe, p. 228.

"perfection, accessibility, and quantity.": Wallace, p. 149.

"There is no doubt . . . *rather* disparagingly!": Wallace, p. 152.

"[T]he boys have dug up . . . in the morning" . . . "tall, rather interesting-looking . . . reputation for honesty.": Wallace, p. 155.

"the liberty to demolish": Letter from William Reed, dated March 14, 1879. http://peabody.yale.edu/collections/vertebrate-paleontology /correspondence-o-c-marsh.

12: SCIENTIFIC SMACKDOWN

"To meet these charges . . . plain words.": Wallace, p. 241.

"using head, tail, and some limb bones . . . the skeleton": Wallace, pp. 158–59.

Cope's Bible: Wallace, p. 175.

Marshiana: Wallace, p. 193.

"SCIENTISTS . . . GEOLOGICAL SURVEY": Jaffe, p. 321.

"gigantic politico-scientific monopoly.": Jaffe, p. 323.

"Either [Marsh] or I must go under . . . to my country" . . . "Has Professor Cope . . . passed judgment.": Johnson, p. 52.

"left him . . . with a genius.": Wallace, p. 265.

"To Yale . . . his estate.": Jaffe, p. 375.

ENDNOTE

Sleeping on a dragon's hoard . . . himself: *The Voyage of the Dawn Treader* by C. S. Lewis, p. 63.

"Marsh was never to have fossils . . . yet more material.": Wallace, p. 144.

Bibliography

* denotes books specifically for young readers

Bates, Marston, and Philip S. Humphrey, eds. *Charles Darwin: An Anthology.* London and New York: Routledge, 2009.

Betts, C. W. "The Yale College Expedition of 1870." *Harper's New Monthly Magazine* vol. XLIII (June to November). New York: Harper & Brothers, 1871.

Calloway, Colin G., ed. *Our Hearts Fell to the Ground: Plains Indian Views of How the West Was Lost.* New York: Bedford/St. Martin's, 1996.

Darwin, Francis, ed. *The Life and Letters of Charles Darwin.* New York: D. Appleton & Co., 1898.

Jaffe, Mark. *The Gilded Dinosaur: The Fossil War Between E. D. Cope and O. C. Marsh and the Rise of American Science.* New York: Crown Publishers, 2000.

*Johnson, Rebecca L. *Battle of the Dinosaur Bones: Othniel Charles Marsh Vs. Edward Drinker Cope.* Minneapolis: Twenty-First Century Books, 2013.

Knight, Charles Robert. *Charles R. Knight: Autobiography of an Artist.* Ann Arbor, Michigan: G.T. Labs, 2005.

Lanham, Url. *The Bone Hunters.* New York: Columbia University Press, 1973.

Marsh, O. C. "Introduction and Succession of Vertebrate Life in America." American Association for the Advancement of Science address, August 30, 1877.

Marsh, O. C. "Thomas Henry Huxley." *The American Journal of Science,* third series, vol. L, nos. 295–300. New Haven: 1895.

Mayor, Adrienne. *Fossil Legends of the First Americans.* Princeton, New Jersey: Princeton University Press, 2005.

Osborn, Henry Fairfield. *Biographical Memoir of Edward Drinker Cope 1840–1897.* Volume XIII-Third Memoir. Washington, DC: National Academy of Sciences, 1929.

Osborn, Henry Fairfield. *Impressions of Great Naturalists: Reminiscences of Darwin, Huxley, Balfour, Cope and Others.* New York: Charles Scribner's Sons, 1924.

Proceedings of the Academy of Natural Sciences of Philadelphia, Volume 21. Philadelphia: 1869.

*Sandler, Martin W. *Iron Rails, Iron Men, and the Race to Link the Nation: The Story of the Transcontinental Railroad.* Somerville, Massachusetts: Candlewick Press, 2015.

Wallace, David Rains. *The Bonehunters' Revenge: Dinosaurs, Greed, and the Greatest Scientific Feud of the Gilded Age.* Boston: Houghton Mifflin, 1999.

Warren, Leonard. *Joseph Leidy: The Last Man Who Knew Everything.* New Haven and London: Yale University Press, 1998.

Weishampel, David B., and Nadine M. White. *The Dinosaur Papers: 1676–1906.* Washington and London: Smithsonian Books, 2003.

FURTHER READING

Davidson, Jane Pierce. *The Bone Sharp: The Life of Edward Drinker Cope.* Philadelphia: Academy of Natural Sciences, 1997.

*Holmes, Thom. Fossil Feud: *The Rivalry of the First American Dinosaur Hunters.* New York: Julian Messner, 1997.

*Kerley, Barbara. *The Dinosaurs of Waterhouse Hawkins.* New York: Scholastic, 2001.

McCarren, Mark J. *The Scientific Contributions of Othniel Charles Marsh: Birds, Bones, and Brontotheres.* New Haven: Peabody Museum of Natural History, Yale University, 1993.

Ostrom, John H., and John S. McIntosh. *Marsh's Dinosaurs: The Collections from Como Bluff.* New Haven: Yale University Press, 2000.

*Ottaviani, Jim. *Bone Sharps, Cowboys, and Thunder Lizards: A Tale of Edward Drinker Cope, Othniel Charles Marsh, and the Gilded Age of Paleontology.* Ann Arbor, Michigan: G.T. Labs, 2005.

Schuchert, Charles and Clara M. LeVene. *O. C. Marsh, Pioneer in Paleontology.* New Haven: Yale University Press, 1940.

WEBLIOGRAPHY

http://academic.brooklyn.cuny.edu/geology/chamber/marsh.html

http://www.ansp.org/exhibits/online-exhibits/stories/crucible-of-the-bone-wars

http://www.cam.ac.uk/research/features
/iggy-the-iguanodon-and-the-160-year-old-dinosaur-song

https://www.darwinproject.ac.uk/letter/DCP-LETT-2544.xml

https://dinotracksdiscovery.org

http://dla.library.upenn.edu/dla/pacscl/ead.html?id=PACSCL_ANSP_ANSPColl328

http://enacademic.com/dic.nsf/enwiki/565381

https://extinctmonsters.net/category/amnh-2/page/3

http://www.lettersofnote.com/2009/09/it-is-like-confessing-murder.html

http://oceansofkansas.com/NYHerald.html

http://peabody.yale.edu/collections/archives/oc-marsh-story

http://peabody.yale.edu/collections/vertebrate-paleontology
/correspondence-o-c-marsh

http://www.rockymountainpaleontology.com/bridger

https://www.smithsonianmag.com/science-nature
/darwin-and-the-dinosaurs-38804133/?no-ist

Acknowledgments

Hatsful of gratitude to my brilliant and meticulous editor, Alex Ulyett, and to everyone at Viking who worked so creatively and diligently to make this book: Kate Renner, Sheila Keenan, Janet Pascal, Ryan Sullivan, and Krista Ahlberg—and to Ken Wright for publishing it.

Mammoth thanks to my friend and agent Jill Grinberg and to the team at Grinberg Literary Management for just . . . everything.

I drew on many sources, but two lively narrative accounts of the Bone War proved indispensable: Mark Jaffe's *The Gilded Dinosaur: The Fossil War Between E. D. Cope and O. C. Marsh and the Rise of American Science* and David Rains Wallace's *The Bonehunters' Revenge: Dinosaurs, Greed, and the Greatest Scientific Feud of the Gilded Age.*

Generous readers combed through early drafts and contributed corrections and clarity. Special thanks to Daniel Brinkman of New Haven, Connecticut; to Hayley Singleton for connecting me with her colleagues John W. Servos and Matthew Inabinett at Amherst College, both of whom offered key insights; and to Alan Zdinak of the Natural History Museum of Los Angeles County. Their help was invaluable, and any remaining errors are my own.

Picture Credits

p. viii: Academy of Natural Sciences of Philadelphia (ANSP) Archives Collection 803; p. 2: Wikimedia Commons; p. 6 (Cope): ANSP Archives; p. 8: Courtesy of the Pennsylvania Academy of Fine Arts, Philadelphia. Gift of Mrs. Sarah Harrison (the Joseph Harrison Collection); p. 9: Wikimedia Commons; p. 12: University Archives and Records Center, University of Pennsylvania; p. 15: Library of Congress Prints and Photographs Division [LC-DIG-ppmsca-07309]; p. 18 (Marsh): Peabody Museum of Natural History, Yale University; pp. 21, 23, 25, 26 (*Hadrosaurus*), and 29: Wikimedia Commons; p. 30: Rijksmuseum, Amsterdam; p. 33: Wikimedia Commons; p. 34: Library of Congress Prints and Photographs Division [LC-DIG-stereo-1s00076]; pp. 37 and 39: Wikimedia Commons; p. 40: RightsLink/Taylor & Francis; p. 42 (Cardiff Giant): Library of Congress Prints and Photographs Division [LC-DIG-ggbain-13790]; p. 45: Wikimedia Commons; pp. 46 and 47 (Crystal Palace dinner): ANSP Archives Collection 803; pp. 48 and 49: Wikimedia Commons; p. 51: Library of Congress Prints and Photographs Division [LC-DIG-cwpbh-04124]; pp. 52, 56, 57 (fire), 60, and 61: author's collection; p. 54: Peabody Museum of Natural History, Yale University; p. 55: Courtesy of Vintage Poster Prints: https://www.etsy.com/shop /VintagePosterPrints; pp. 57 (Buffalo Bill) and 59: Wikimedia Commons; p. 63: *[Pteranodon longiceps? Marsh, 1876],* [YPM VP 000346] Courtesy, Division of Vertebrate Paleontology, Peabody Museum of Natural History, Yale University; p. 64: American Museum of Natural History (AMNH), Library; p. 67: Wikimedia Commons; p. 69: AMNH, Library; p. 72: Peabody Museum of Natural History, Yale University; p. 74: © Deborah Noyes/courtesy of Peabody Museum of Natural History, Yale University; p. 77: AMNH, Library; p. 78: ANSP Archives; p. 81: Library of Congress Prints and Photographs Division [LC-USZ62-101767]; p. 82: AMNH, Library; p. 85: Library of Congress Prints and Photographs Division [LC-USZ62-91032]; p. 86: Wikimedia Commons; p. 89: Peabody Museum of Natural History, Yale University; p. 90: Wikimedia Commons; p. 91 (Custer): Library of Congress Prints and Photographs Division [LC-DIG-cwpbh-03110]; p. 91 (Sitting Bull): Library of Congress Prints and Photographs Division [LC-DIG-ppmsca-39879]; p. 92: Library of Congress Prints and Photographs Division [LC-DIG-ppmsc-02600]; p. 94: Library of Congress Geography and Map Division [75694669]; p. 96: Wikimedia Commons; p. 98: AMNH, Library; p. 100: ALAMY; p. 101: Peabody Museum of Natural History, Yale University; p. 104: Courtesy of the Royal Gorge Regional Museum & History Center, Cañon City, CO; p. 106: [Othniel Charles Marsh papers, 1817–1899 (inclusive) [45376] Courtesy of Manuscripts & Archives, Yale University; p. 107: ALAMY; p. 109: Wikimedia Commons; pp. 112 and 113: Peabody Museum of Natural History, Yale University; p. 114: ALAMY; p. 116: ANSP; p. 118: John Margolies Roadside America photograph archive (1972-2008), Library of Congress, Prints and Photographs Division LC-MA05- 3606 [P&P]; p. 123: Library of Congress, Prints & Photographs Division [LC-USZ62-60721]; p. 124: Wikimedia Commons

Index

Note: Page numbers in *italics* indicate images and captions.